1999

TRANSFORMING SCHOOLS INTO COMMUNITY LEARNING CENTERS

Steve R. Parson

Virginia Tech
Blacksburg, Virginia

EYE ON EDUCATION
6 DEPOT WAY WEST, SUITE 106
LARCHMONT, NY 10538
(914) 833–0551
(914) 833–0761 fax

Library of Congress Cataloging-in-Publication Data

Parson, Steve R.
        Transforming schools into community learning centers / by Steve R. Parson.
        p.   cm.
        Includes bibliographical references and indexes.
        ISBN 1-883001-61-7
        1. Community schools—United States. 2. Community and school—United States. 3. School improvement programs—United States. I. Title.
LB2820.P37   1999
371.19'0973—dc21   98–35987
                                                                                CIP
10 9 8 7 6 5 4 3 2 1

Editorial and production services provided by Richard H. Adin Freelance Editorial Services, 9 Orchard Drive, Gardiner, NY 12525 (914-883-5884)

Also Available from EYE ON EDUCATION

Data Analysis for Comprehensive
Schoolwide Improvement
by Victoria L. Bernhardt

The School Portfolio:
A Comprehensive Framework for School Improvement
by Victoria L. Bernhardt

Innovations in Parent and Family Involvement
by J. Wiliam Rioux and Nancy Berla

School-To-Work
by Arnold H. Packer and Marion W. Pines

The Administrator's Guide to School
Community Relations
by George E. Pawlas

Handbook of Educational Terms and Applications
by Arthur K. Ellis and Jeffrey T. Fouts

The Educator's Brief Guide to the Internet
and the World Wide Web
by Eugene F. Provenzo, Jr.

The Principal as Steward
by Jack McCall

The Principal's Edge
by Jack McCall

Research on Educational Innovations, 2d ed.
by Arthur K. Ellis and Jeffrey T. Fouts

Research on School Restructuring
by Arthur K. Ellis and Jeffrey T. Fouts

MEET THE AUTHOR

Steve Parson is Associate Professor in the Department of Educational Leadership and Policy Studies at Virginia Tech. He heads an initiative to develop an Urban Institute for Partnership Development with the National Association of Partners in Education, the ERIC Clearinghouse on Urban Education, Columbia University, and Virginia Tech.

Formerly a Mott Intern with the Western Michigan University Community Education Leadership Program, he has served as president of the National Community Association. He is also a consultant and trainer in the field of community education, educational partnerships and educational reform.

TABLE OF CONTENTS

INTRODUCTION

America needs a new vision for its public schools, a vision that will change the way the local school is viewed and the role it plays in the community. This new vision is ready to emerge, but few educators or policymakers have looked at the process of change from a systemic perspective. Our reform efforts tend to focus on fixing one problem at a time, not viewing the school as part of a larger system; that is, the community served by the school. What is proposed here is a new way of thinking about public schools.

As this book is written, public schools continue to be pressured to undergo a major transformation. Several waves of educational reform have swept the country in recent years, most of them powered by a perceived national crisis.

Major restructuring and changes are taking place in virtually all of our nation's economic, governmental, political, religious, and educational institutions. In education, some schools are changing from the traditional seven-period day to block scheduling in which students take fewer classes for longer periods of the school day. Some schools are moving toward the controversial outcomes-based education, and some have eliminated ability tracking as a way to organize students for instruction. There are schools in which cooperative learning and problem-based learning methods are being tried, and in which special education students are being taught in regular classrooms. And the list goes on.

A great deal of interest in schools becoming Community Learning Centers has been generated by the current administration of President Bill Clinton and Secretary of Education Richard Riley. Funding for the Department of Education's 21st Century Community Learning Centers Program is estimated to be nearly $2 billion over a five-year span beginning in 1999. This program, while advocating a broader role for traditional schools, primarily focuses on using schools as sites for quality after-school care for America's children.

From my perspective, none of these changes alone represents genuine restructuring. Each may be worthwhile and may actually improve the quality of education, but not one addresses the kind of comprehensive, systemic restructuring that I believe is needed if our schools are to respond to the challenges of the coming century.

In a class discussion of charter schools and whether or not they could serve as catalysts for change, one student noted that most charter schools are free from the rules and regulations that govern other public schools. Not everyone, however, agreed that this freedom, of itself, guarantees improvement. One student, a talented young principal, said, "We already have a lot of freedom in my school system, but I don't know where we would change what we are currently doing." We are all prisoners of the current paradigm that tells us what schools should be and how they should function. The advantage of creating charter schools is that the founders can start from ground zero, without preconceived notions of what must be included. The charter is a license to create a new paradigm.

While this book is not specifically about charter schools, it offers a strategy for communities that want to redesign their schools from the bottom up. Note the term *communities*. Communities, not educators, politicians, parents, or policymakers, must want to change. Schools are an integral part of a community system, and to change them in a meaningful way requires the collaborative efforts of the entire community. That is what this book is about—how community members can work together to redesign their schools to meet community needs and more nearly realize their full potential.

Newman (1992, p. 31) identified several building blocks for restructuring schools:

- Student experiences.
- Professional life of teachers.
- School governance, management, and leadership.
- Coordination of community resources

These building blocks provide much of the framework for the changes advocated in *Transforming Schools into Community Learning Centers*.

The theoretical base for much of this book may be found in the work of John Dewey, Joseph K. Hart, Jack Minzey and Clyde LeTarte, Joyce Epstein, Michael Fullan, Larry and Virginia Decker, Maurice Seay, Donald Weaver, and others. I also draw heavily on my experience as a Mott Intern in Flint, Michigan, in the early 1970s, and my involvement over more than two decades in the worldwide Community Education Development Network.

The concept of the community school is certainly not a new one. Seay and Crawford (1954, pp. 13–14), in writing about the early development of community schools in Flint, Michigan, identified two distinct characteristics that set those schools apart from the traditional schools of their day:

◆ Service was rendered to the entire community, not just to children of school age.

◆ The discovery, development, and use of community resources became an integral part of the school's instructional facilities and programs.

The vision presented here suggests focal points for change, offering a process for continuous adjustment as community and societal needs change. It is foolish to present a one-size-fits-all approach to school restructuring. Each school and each community has its own distinctive character, and mix of resources, problems, and needs. What I offer is a process that enables schools to

◆ Develop a consensus on what services the community school should provide and how they should be provided.

◆ Use the total resources of the community to improve the quality of education.

◆ Help the community to become self-actualized in its development as a good place to live and raise children.

Throughout the book you will find examples of currently functioning Community Learning Centers.

This book is addressed to a broad audience. First, it is for teachers and school administrators who are now on the front-line of the process of changing schools from the inside out. Second, it is for the many committed parents and community members who want to be involved in redesigning their schools. Third, it is for the business and corporate community, which has a real stake in the outcome of school reform and increasingly wants to be a part of the action. Finally, it is for the university faculties who are responsible for preparing the leaders of tomorrow's schools.

The collective action of all these groups is required to bring about the kind of change proposed in these pages. Some chapters may be of more interest to some readers than to others, but every reader should examine the totality of the ideas presented, rather than focusing on a single aspect.

I would like to think that this book will never be finished. As you read and think about Community Learning Centers, I hope you will enter in a dialogue with me about how to continue refining and improving this agenda as we learn more about how Community Learning Centers work or don't work in the real world. John Dewey (1933, p. 224) wrote: "It does not pay to tether one's thoughts to the post of use with too short a rope. Power in action requires largeness of vision, which can be had only through the use of imagination." Together, we can pool our imagination to create a new vision of schools for the twenty-first century.

The dialogue I propose can take place electronically through that powerful tool, the Internet. I hope to hear about your experiences, the successful Community Learning Center models you have observed, and your ideas about how we might initiate the change process. This dialogue will keep the ideas contained in this book fresh and relevant.

My e-mail address is **parson@vt.edu**. I look forward to hearing from you.

REFERENCES

Newman, F. 1992. "A Developing Design," in A Leader's Guide to School Restructuring. Reston, VA: National Association of Secondary School Principals.

Seay, M. And Crawford, F. 1954. The Community School and Community Self Improvement. Lansing, MI: State Department of Public Instruction.

1

TRANSFORMING OUR SCHOOLS

Good educators must be able to build bridges for students to cross over and then collapse them to allow [students] to build their own bridges.

Unknown Greek philosopher

There was a time when school books were the resting place of all the answers, and we all knew that. Students would read with highlighter in hand, trying to guess which parts were the most important. Of course, "most important" translated into what was going to be on the next test.

This book is not a textbook in the traditional sense. There is no teacher's edition, and there are no test questions that correspond with the content. There is, however, a very real test involved with this book: Are communities willing to and capable of coming together to redesign their schools as Community Learning Centers? We do have a pretty good idea that the school as we know it, in its present form, will not survive long into the twenty-first century.

No Blueprints

As this book began to take form, some thought was given to asking an architect to produce detailed drawings to depict what a Community Learning Center building might look like. But as the work progressed, it became clear that the Community Learning Center was not about buildings. It was about people, programs, and processes working together to create the culture of a learning organization that would serve entire communities, replacing traditional elementary and secondary schools. In the words of the unknown philosopher quoted at the beginning of this chapter, we must build bridges for students and then collapse them so that students can build their own bridges. That calls for a rather unusual blueprint.

If there were a blueprint relevant to this book, it might look more like a road map, laying out directions for turning a traditional school into a Community Learning Center. The blueprint for each Center would require custom designing that addresses the problems and opportunities offered by the community it is going to serve. This chapter begins to develop that blueprint and provides suggestions for putting the change process into motion.

Assumptions About Change

Two magnitudes of change have been used to categorize changes that have taken place in education. First-order changes have aimed at improving the efficiency or effectiveness of what is already in place, without making any fundamental change in the structure and process. Second-order changes have tried to change the structure of the organization, its goals, values, and ways of doing business.

> First-order changes succeed while second-order changes are either adapted to fit what existed or sloughed off, allowing the system to remain essentially untouched. The ingredients change, the Chinese saying goes, but the soup remains the same. (Cuban 1988, p. 343)

The successful transition from a traditional school to a Community Learning Center represents a second-order change that will change the traditional school organization, goals, and processes in fundamental ways.

Some of the early work of Michael Fullan (1991) provides a good framework for addressing the process of change that can guide the development of the Community Learning Center. Fullan believes that certain assumptions are basic to a successful approach to educational change. These assumptions together provide the foundation for developing a Community Learning Center. Each assumption is discussed briefly here.

ASSUMPTION 1: TRANSFORMATION REQUIRES THE DEVELOPMENT AND FREE EXCHANGE OF IDEAS

This is a book of ideas. It contains no cookbook recipe or fixed model of what a Community Learning Center in a community should look like when it has completed its transformation from a traditional school. There are two reasons for this. First, no two communities are exactly alike, and therefore no two Community Learning Centers will look exactly alike. The needs and resources residing in each community dictate what the Center looks like. Second, no Community Learning Center should ever be viewed as a finished product. Centers should always be in a stage of evolving. This dynamic nature is necessary to meet the year-to-year, or even day-to-day, fluid conditions that exist in the community.

ASSUMPTION 2: IMPLEMENTERS WHO WORK IN GROUPS WILL PRODUCE THE BEST RESULTS

To accomplish any level of innovation requires people who are willing to take risks. These people cannot expect to work in isolation if they hope to bring about the kind of change represented in the concept of the Community Learning Center. Individual implementers have to come together to share their ideas and develop a shared view of what could be. The size of the group need not be large, but there will be a higher level of success if there is good representation from all the stakeholder groups involved in a typical school. This means that teachers, administrators, students, parents, and community members must be welcomed among the innovators.

ASSUMPTION 3: CONFLICT AND DISAGREEMENT ARE INEVITABLE

Most of us have been raised to avoid conflict. We spend an inordinate amount of time and energy trying to avoid conflict and eliminate disagreement. The reality is that in issues that really matter to people, conflict and disagreement are natural phenomena. Crawley (1992) uses the term "constructive conflict" as a way of encouraging us to view conflict in a positive light. He suggests that in a world in which high value is placed on individual achievement, with emphasis on competition and the pursuit of self-interest, great effort is required on the part of leaders to develop constructive methods for resolving differences. To be able to consider the many different constituencies in any community, leaders must learn to value and appreciate conflict as a natural occurrence, as natural to human beings as taking a breath.

ASSUMPTION 4: PEOPLE NEED PRESSURE IN ORDER TO CHANGE

The pressure to change comes from interaction with others who are open to change, from the sense of being empowered to make decisions about change, and from technical assistance. If people in the community are given power to make decisions about their own Community Learning Center, that alone will create a potent pressure for change. Technical assistance may come in the form of knowledgeable people available to help, or it may be data about the community, or the vision of models created in other communities. To create real change, people will have to involve themselves in the process of relearning what they already know about schools and communities.

ASSUMPTION 5: REAL CHANGE TAKES TIME

Experiences in educational change lead us to believe that specific innovations often take two to three years to implement, and many institutional reforms may take five years or more to complete. A significant investment of time is required to transform a traditional school into a Community Learning Center. For those of us who are short on patience, it is not an easy process. But change must be thought of as a developmental process that is tested through practice. Persistence is critical to being able to stay with the change process long enough to begin to produce tangible results.

ASSUMPTION 6: LACK OF PROGRESS MAY HAVE MANY CAUSES

A lack of progress should not be attributed solely to a rejection of the values embodied in the change, or to a rejection of change itself. There may be many reasons for a lack of progress, including a rejection of values, a lack of resources, or not allowing sufficient time for implementation of change.

ASSUMPTION 7: NOT EVERYONE WILL CHANGE

All changes start with a small circle of implementers. As small successes are experienced, the circle widens. A widening of the circle takes place throughout the change process. Not everyone will join the circle in support of innovation, however. Every community has some people who resist change no matter what is taking place. These resisters tend to fall into one of two categories. First, there are the critics. They will not get involved, sometimes even declining to learn what innovations are being proposed. Second, there are the blockers. Blockers work at obstructing anything that upsets the status quo. Of the two groups, the blockers are far more detrimental to change than the critics. Change can take place in spite of the critics, but too often the blockers are able to obstruct change or even sabotage it after it is in place. There are times when the best solution for dealing with the blockers, if they cannot be brought into the circle of implementers, is to help them find a work setting that better matches their view of the world.

A PLAN IS NEEDED

The change process requires a long-range plan to deal with all of these assumptions; leave nothing to chance. The plan must be comprehensive, and yet allow for the evolution-ary nature of the change process. It cannot remain fixed in its original form. Make adjustments on a regular basis in order to accommodate the inevitable changes that take place in the community.

Changing the Culture of Institutions

If we get caught up in adopting innovations such as com-munity partnerships, we may lose sight of the real challenge — changing the culture of the school itself. Merely fine tuning what is already in place is to remain at the first-order level of change. To approach the level of change represented by the Community Learning Center, it is necessary to address the to-tal culture of today's schools.

Elizabeth and Gifford Pinchot (1996, pp. 9–10) identified five distinct organizational roles to foster the process of inno-vation. Filling these roles is critical to the successful develop-ment of the Community Learning Center.

- The idea person or inventor to encourage the cre-ativity that lies within each person.

- The intrapreneur or hands-on-champion. This is the person in an institution who is given the free-dom and resources to take bright ideas (his or her own, or that of others) from concept to actuality.

- The collaborative, cross-functional, intrapreneur-ial team of volunteers recruited by the lead intra-preneur. The team stays with the project from its early stages through implementation.

- The sponsor or executive champion whose close relationship to the intrapreneurial team guides the project around obstacles and intervenes with the hierarchy to keep it alive.

- The climate maker, who creates a climate sup-portive of innovation.

WHAT IS A COMMUNITY LEARNING CENTER?

A community learning center can be developed from a traditional school in a traditional school building in any community. It could be built from the ground up, as we find in the case of many of the charter school models. But, there are several components that will be found in common in community learning centers.

- ♦ Services are provided to the whole community in addition to focusing on the educational needs of the children.
- ♦ Community resources become a regular part of the instructional program.
- ♦ Community services for families and children work together in the community learning center to provide needed programs and services.
- ♦ People from throughout the community can gain access to technology in the community learning center.
- ♦ Leadership is shared among all the community stakeholders.

Throughout this book you will find these components repeated as themes for the transformation of traditional schools into community learning centers.

THE PLAN

Each community has to devise its own plan, but there are common elements that need to be addressed. The plan that follows should be viewed as an example of what needs to be addressed as the transformation of the school occurs.

A COMMUNITY THAT WANTS TO IMPROVE EDUCATION

Are people willing to get involved in creating a climate for improving the quality of education for everyone in the community? Is there community interest in creating a Community Learning Center? These questions must be addressed at the very beginning of the process. Communitywide forums might be conducted for people to get together to talk about education in the community, and to be exposed to the concept of a Community Learning Center instead of a school. All it takes at this point is to have a cadre of people who are willing to say, "It sounds interesting. Let's find out more."

AN AGREEMENT ON HOW DECISIONS ARE TO BE MADE

There must be a commitment to widespread inclusion in the decision-making process. This is one of the building blocks for the Community Learning Center, so it must be a part of the culture from the very beginning. Some sort of representative group needs to be established to provide leadership during the transformation process. In schools in which there is already a structure for shared decision-making, such as a school management council or school improvement team, the organization already in place may be used to guide the development of a new structure. It is extremely important that the new group includes all of the significant stakeholders in the community:

- Teachers and support staff
- Parents and students
- Administrators
- Community leaders and business people
- Community service agency staff

OBTAINING THE RESOURCES NEEDED TO SUPPORT A PLANNING PROCESS

To be successful, the planning process must have an adequate resource base to support it during the early stages. Costs will be incurred in facilitating involvement in the development of a plan. Costs might include the purchase of books and materials, travel, printing and postage, and the assistance of consultants. Sources of funding for this early stage might be:

+ Grants from private foundations.
+ Federal and state grants (in some states, Goals 2000 funds might be available).
+ Funds from corporate partners.
+ Funds from school support groups (PTA, booster clubs, etc.).
+ Funds from community service clubs (Junior League, Kiwanis, Rotary, etc.).
+ Contributions from local government.

The chart on the next page shows some examples of the costs incurred in establishing Community Learning Center programs in three schools. In addition to the total cost, the sources of funding are identified.

DEFINING THE ROLE OF THE LEADERSHIP GROUP

As the process begins, time is an enemy. Frequent meetings are needed, and time must be found to include a representative group of people in determining the direction and strategies needed for the transformation. Creative means must be found to facilitate the participation of all stakeholder representatives on the leadership team. Some ideas that have worked are:

+ Provide a small stipend for all participants.
+ Provide release time during the school day.
+ Incorporate some planning time into the school schedule.
+ Hold meetings in the evenings.

Some sacrifices are required of those who become involved in the leadership of the transformation. Most are willing to make the necessary sacrifices when they believe that what they are doing will truly make a difference in the quality of life and education in their community.

ESTABLISHING STUDY GROUPS

A number of study groups, including all of the stakeholder groups, need to meet regularly to examine the concept

SAMPLE COST AND FUNDING FOR THREE SUCCESSFUL COMMUNITY LEARNING CENTER PROGRAMS

St. Louis Public Schools (MO)	Murfreesboro Schools (TN)	The Virtual Y, New York City (NY)
Serves: 16 school-based Community Education Centers serving 44,000 residents each year. An average of 70–90 kids each day.	**Serves:** 9 elementary schools, with a total enrollment of 5,400 (K-8). 80% of the kids participate during the year; 500–600 of Cason Lane Academy's 950 kids participate every day.	**Serves:** Will operate in 240 schools, serving over 10,000 students. Fifty 2nd to 4th graders per school will participate daily.
Offers: Tutoring, arts, and recreation, adult classes, drug-prevention programs.	**Offers:** Optional full-day schedule, enrichment, arts and recreation.	**Offers:** Homework assistance, tutoring, values and substance abuse education, arts and recreation; focuses on literacy.
Funding: Fees for adult classes; HUD block grant; school board supplement.	**Funding:** Regular budget plus grants plus fees of $1.25/hour plus materials.	**Funding:** Private sponsors for direct and administrative costs.
Year Total: $102,250	**Year Total:** $200,00 at Cason Lane Academy	**Year Total:** $25,000 per site + administrative costs shared by all sites.

Source: U.S. Department of Education
http://www.gov/pubs/LearnCenters/finance.html

of a Community Learning Center. These study groups will involve people who are interested enough in making changes to invest some time in studying what changes might work in their local school. The study groups might identify a common set of readings, so that everyone has the same background. Group members might be encouraged to make trips to other communities that are involved in making similar changes in their schools. University faculty members could be recruited to serve as facilitators of these study groups.

CREATING COMMUNITYWIDE AWARENESS

The study groups can be involved in developing programs to explain to the entire community what they have learned about Community Learning Centers. These programs could use a variety of ways to reach people in the community.

- Forums held in churches, community centers, and community meeting rooms in local shopping malls.

- Presentations on community-access cable television channels.

- Videotapes available by loan at community libraries and videotape stores.

- Plays designed to portray life in the Community Learning Center with student and community members in the cast.

- Community Learning Center Transformation newsletters produced by students and community members.

- Articles in community newspapers.

- Appearances on local television interview shows.

- Bulletins posted on electronic networks in the community.

- An Internet home page for the Community Learning Center Transformation.

HELP FOR THE JOURNEY

Community education has always been a journey, not a destination. As communities begin this journey, they should know that they are not traveling alone. Across the country, and in many parts of the world, there is a rising movement toward community education as a way of transforming schools and communities into places where all community residents can thrive and grow and reach their full potential.

A growing resource base is available to assist communities in this transformational process. Throughout the rest of this book are numerous of examples of how communities have implemented various aspects of the Community Learning Center. In the Appendix, a list of resource agencies and organizations is provided to assist in building Community Learning Centers. People, working together, can make a difference in their communities. Together, they must begin the journey to create the kind of learning community we need to face the challenges of the new century.

REFERENCES

Crawley, John. 1994. *Constructive Conflict Management*. San Diego: Pfeiffer & Co.

Cuban, Larry. 1988. "A Fundamental Puzzle of School Reform," *Phi Delta Kappan*, 70(5), 341–44.

Fullan, Michael G. 1991. *The Meaning of Educational Change*. New York: Teachers College Press.

Pinchot, Gifford, and Elizabeth Pinchot. 1996. "Five Drivers of Innovation," *Executive Excellence*, 13(1), 9–10.

2

COMMUNITY LEARNING CENTERS

As I was developing the Community Learning Center concept, I was frequently asked why I did not use the term "school" or "community school." My answer is this: Our society has had such a long history with schools and schooling that it makes sense, if we are to create a major change in the institution of the school, to invent a new name, which communicates more clearly the kind of institution that would evolve from that change.

One difficulty that is encountered when comparing the Community Learning Center with the traditional school is that no two schools or communities are precisely alike, so there is no "typical" school. Even so, traditional schools have common characteristics. This chapter describes schools as we now know them in order to develop a context for the changes that are necessary to create Community Learning Centers.

WHY DO WE NEED TO CHANGE?

In the Phi Delta Kappa (1994) videotape series *Reinventing Our Schools*, Phillip Schlechty, director of the Center for Leadership in School Reform, said, "There is one group that believes that schools have somehow deteriorated and gotten worse than they used to be. Another group argues that schools are better at doing what they used to do but it doesn't want them to do those same things any more." Schlechty counts himself among the latter group, believing that schools are not doing too badly but that they need to redesign what they are doing and focus on change. Many prefer to think of schools as needing to be restructured, rather than reformed, because "reform" evokes images of the wayward, in need of redemption.

The public schools in this nation have well-served children and young people over the years, but they have also grown distant from the communities they serve. There are many reasons for this: growth in the size of individual school units; state and federal mandates; educators' mistrust of community members; community mistrust of educators; demographic shifts in the makeup of the family; and a focus on "schooling," rather than on education.

As Minzey and LeTarte (1994, p. xiii) put it, "There is still a need for a major change in education, not just in rearranging the current program but in restructuring the very nature of schools and actually redefining and altering the current paradigm we call public education." Public schools must connect with the communities they serve to take on the difficult job of providing opportunities for all children, youth, and adults to realize their full potential. Schools are now becoming aware that they can neither do the job alone nor continue to exist as islands apart from their communities.

More than half a century ago, William Carr (1942, p. 34) painted a striking picture of schools as islands in their communities:

> Many schools are like little islands set apart from the mainland of life by a deep moat of convention and tradition. Across this moat there is a drawbridge which is lowered at certain periods during the day in order that the part-time inhabitants may cross over to the island in the morning and back to the mainland at night. Why do these young people go out to the island? They go there in order to learn

how to live on the mainland. When they reach the island, they are provided with a supply of excellent books that tell about life on the mainland. They read these books diligently, even memorizing parts of them. Then they take examinations on them.

Once in a while, as a special treat, the bus takes a few of the more fortunate or favored islanders on a hasty tour through the mainland itself. But this is very rare and is allowed to occur when the reading of the books about the mainland has been thoroughly completed.

After the last inhabitant has left in the early afternoon, the drawbridge is raised. Janitors clean up the island, and the lights go out....It never occurs to anyone on the mainland to go to the island after the usual daylight hours. The drawbridge stays up and the island is left empty and lifeless through all the late afternoon and evening hours, all the early morning hours, and all day on Saturday and Sunday.

Day after day, week after week, continues the strange procession of young people going out to the island to learn about life on the mainland.

Unfortunately, Carr could go into many of our communities today and find schools still operating in virtually the same way. This book seeks to provide a vision of schools as institutions that are no longer islands designed exclusively for children, but have become genuine learning centers for everyone in the community.

THE VISION OF COMMUNITY LEARNING CENTERS

About five years ago, I participated in a dialogue at the National Center for Community Education in Flint, Michigan. The purpose was to develop a vision of what the community school of the twenty-first century should look like. The group was composed of two dozen people from the community education movement in the United States and Canada; universities, local school districts, and state departments of education were represented.

The vision developed by the group included many of the characteristics of the community schools that have been developed in North America over the last two or three decades. But few, if any, of the vision schools embodied the concept of community-centered learning taking place throughout the school.

The community school envisioned during the dialogue session has these features:

+ It is open year-round, day and night.
+ It serves all ages, often in intergenerational programs.
+ Decision-making involves the community.
+ The building has a multiuse design.
+ The curriculum is community-based.
+ The school serves as a community technology center.
+ The school has partnerships in and with the community.
+ Its system of governance is community designed.
+ The community supports the school.
+ Everyone is both teacher and learner.
+ Risk-takers are willing to fail and try again.
+ Mentors for students are recruited from the community.
+ The level of parent and family involvement is high.

This vision of the community school of the twenty-first century has been my guide in developing the concept of the Community Learning Center—a concept that cuts across a wide range of issues in the design and operation of a school. The concept is not, of course, entirely new. Its historical roots can be found in the progressive education movement of John Dewey (1916) and the writings of Samuel Everett (1938) and his colleagues in *The Community School*. In the 1930s, the Mott Foundation, in partnership with the Flint, Michigan, public schools, developed the prototype of the community school that exists today in communities across North America. A few years ago, the Bush administration established the New American Schools Development Corporation (NASDC) to support the development of "break the mold" schools that would lead the restructuring movement then underway. One of the nine original design teams proposed a Community Learning Center model (InfoMedia, 1994) that has many of the characteristics identified by the dialogue group that met at the National Community Education Center. All of these designs owe something to the concept of community schools developed in the United States in the early 1900s.

COMPARING THE DIFFERENCES

In comparing the traditional school with the Community Learning Center, these dimensions will be used: time; space; relationship to other organizations and agencies; family/ community involvement; instruction; use of technology; and sources of leadership. These dimensions provide the framework for contrasting the differences between schools as we know them and the Community Learning Centers proposed for the future.

TIME

Traditional School	*Community Learning Center*
5 days a week	7 days a week
6–8 hours a day	10–12 hours a day
180–200 days a year	300+ days a year
50-minute class periods	Extended blocks of time

The concept of year-round operation of the Community Learning Center is examined in Chapter 9. There are many compelling reasons for discontinuing the antiquated practice of closing schools during the summer months. The traditional September-to-June school calendar arose in an agricultural age, when youth labor was needed in the fields and barns of the family farm. Now, less than three percent of U.S.

families live on farms, and mechanization has decreased the need for youth manpower in most kinds of agriculture.

If General Motors were ordered to operate its plants less than 75 percent of the time, shutting down its operation every summer, the management would be quick to point out that they have an obligation to realize a return on the stockholders' investment in those plants; using them at less than their full capacity would diminish that return. Why, then, are we willing to close one of the largest public investments, the schools, for more than two months every summer? Should we not feel an obligation to the taxpayers who support our public schools and attempt to maximize the return on their investment?

I do not propose that we extend the school year by doing more of the same things we are currently doing, or that we adopt a rotating schedule that would simply use the buildings year round without increasing the amount of time each student spends in school. What I propose is that schools, operating year round, provide students with those activities and services they are unable to provide under the present abbreviated school calendar.

Community Learning Centers are open and available to the community seven days a week in the morning, afternoon, and evening. This seven-day operation recognizes that not all members of the community have the same schedules or the same religious observances. The goal is to operate at full capacity with programs and services designed to meet the broadly defined needs of the whole community.

SPACE

Traditional School	*Community Learning Center*
Education takes place in the classroom.	Education takes place throughout the community.

The Community Learning Center redefines the space and location in which learning takes place and the resources that are brought into the teaching and learning process. Responsibility for education is accepted by both the community and the school. William A. Yeager (1939, pp. 3–4), an early critic of American education, wrote eloquently about what the nature of that relationship should be: "Education conceived as a cooperative process entails responsibilities upon all of those concerned in the educational process. As the eye cannot get along without the hand, neither can the school get along without the home, nor the school or the home without the community."

This transformation of schools involves a recognition that authentic education may take place outside the four walls of the classroom, in such places in the community as zoos, museums, nursing homes, homeless shelters, hospitals, the mayor's office, and so forth.

RELATIONSHIP TO OTHER AGENCIES AND ORGANIZATIONS

Traditional School	*Community Learning Center*
Few connections with other community agencies and organizations.	Collaboration with other community agencies to provide services to families and children.

The Community Learning Center also serves as a focal point for the delivery of critical services to families and children. This does not mean that public schools should become providers of all these services, but rather that they provide a place in each community where community members can come for services delivered by appropriate community agencies and organizations.

"The physical, financial, and human resources of every community should be interconnected and used to their fullest if the diverse needs and interests of the community are to be met," Larry Decker and associates (1990, p. 11) write in *Community Education: Building Learning Communities*. Schools have to be thought of as part of a larger system in the community.

FAMILY AND COMMUNITY INVOLVEMENT

Traditional School	*Community Learning Center*
Involvement limited to parent participation in such activities as open houses and parent conferences.	A comprehensive process of family and community involvement in a wide range of programs and activities.

Probably no education issue has received more attention in recent years than parent, family, and community involvement. The term used is intentionally broad so as to include the breadth of stakeholders who are potentially affected by the outcome of public education efforts and who have the ability to influence the educational process itself.

Parents are beginning to be widely recognized as a child's first teachers. They are also being acknowledged as having the best knowledge of and insight into each individual child. Yet, many schools have failed to develop a comprehensive plan to involve families and parents, and most school budgets offer little evidence that significant resources are devoted to parent, family, and community involvement.

At the national level, the adoption of a strategic plan for the Department of Education initiative, the Family Involvement Partnership for Learning, brought together branches of the federal government and a variety of nongovernmental organizations and associations committed to improving the quality of education for all children. This new partnership signals the beginning of an era in which the family's role in the learning process is brought to the forefront of education reform. The goals adopted by the national partnership are listed in Chapter 4.

The positive impact of parent involvement has been well documented. The research of Epstein (1986, 1987, 1991, 1993), Davies (1988, 1991), and others, clearly show that student achievement improves when parents get involved in their children's education. It would seem natural for schools to concentrate on this proven approach to improving student learning. The reality is that, with a few notable exceptions, educators are talking a lot about parents but doing little to get them involved. The Community Learning Center has a comprehensive and continuous program to engage parents, families, and the community in the teaching and learning process.

INSTRUCTION

Traditional School	*Community Learning Center*
One teacher lectures to a homogeneous group of students.	Teams of teachers work with groups of students of varying abilities.
Emphasis is on paper-and-pencil, norm-referenced tests.	Authentic assessment is used to test whether students can use their knowledge in real-world situations.
Instruction is limited to resources represented by the teacher and the textbooks.	Instruction uses resources from the community.
Students focus on individual assignments.	Collaborative methods teach students how to work as members of a team.

John Goodlad (1984, p. 109) provides a depressing description of instruction in a traditional school:

> Teachers talk at pupils; students work on written assignments or answer specific narrow questions; there is little feedback or guidance from the teacher; students work with textbooks and complete written homework assignments, and are judged by how well they perform on paper and pencil tests.

As we begin restructuring our work at the university where I teach (yes, higher education is addressing the process of change, too!), we are moving away from the traditional lecture, test, term paper format. Now, we often teach as members of a team, using collaborative methods and measuring student learning through authentic assessments designed to show how well the student can perform when faced with realistic situations from the world in which they live and work. We jokingly say we are moving from "the sage on the stage" to "the guide on the side." This approach to teaching and learning characterizes the new Community Learning Center.

The Community Learning Center supports the formation of teacher teams to work with students who, in most cases, are grouped heterogeneously. These teacher teams will facilitate student learning through teaching approaches that are based on collaborative or cooperative learning, using inquiry and problem-based approaches that will allow students to acquire knowledge and to apply what they learn.

Learning will be assessed by giving students opportunities to show how well they can perform tasks using what they have learned in the classroom. Resources from the community will be used to support classroom instruction. On many occasions, classes go into the community to take advantage of community resources that cannot be brought into the school.

USE OF TECHNOLOGY

Traditional School	*Community Learning Center*
Instructional technology is centered in media centers and computer labs.	Instructional technology is located throughout the school.
Technology hardware is reserved for student use only, and only during the regular school day.	Technology hardware is available for student, family, and community use.
A few specialists are trained to use instructional technology.	All teachers, staff, and students have the skills to make use of multimedia technology. Networks give all classrooms access to the Internet.
There is little access to telecommunications resources such as the Internet.	
Except for videotapes, televised instruction is not part of the school's program.	Interactive two-way televised instruction is used to enrich curriculum offerings for all students and the community.

The use of technology provides a dramatic demarcation between the traditional school and the Community Learning Center. The key difference is access. The Community Learning Center makes all forms of instructional technology available to students, faculty, staff, and even to parents and community members. This takes detailed planning and a greater investment than communities have been willing to make in the past. Support from the community will be increased by demonstrating a commitment to making access to new technology a reality for everyone in the community.

In a recent graduate class for school leaders, the faculty teaching team had invited the superintendent of a nearby school district to talk about how technology was being used to improve instruction in his schools. The superintendent warned that schools need to be ready for students who will enter school already computer literate. He used the example of his own two-year-old who uses one of the two computers in their home to play simple educational games. What struck me as I listened to him was the gulf between his child and some other child a mile or two down the road in a low-income housing project, with no computer and few books or magazines suitable for children. I believe that we will soon face a serious gap between children who have access to technology at home and those who do not. Having a place in the community where children, parents, and families can regularly go to make use of technology will lessen the effect on learning of this gap in access. All we have to do is find ways to make use of equipment that is now locked up after the last school bus leaves the front drive of the school.

(Text continues on next page.)

LEADERSHIP

Traditional School	Community Learning Center
Decisions are made by central office staff or by principals.	Decision making is a shared responsibility of principals, teachers, staff, parents, students, and members of the school community. Leadership is shared among all stakeholders in the school community, who are held jointly accountable for results.
Principals are expected to be leaders of their schools and are held accountable for results.	
Parents and the community have no voice in developing plans for the school or in deciding how resources will be used.	Parents and the community have multiple opportunities to be involved in developing an annual plan and deciding how resources are to be used.

A new form of leadership is taking shape in many schools. Individual schools and school districts may call it site-based management, school-based improvement, or shared decision-making. Whatever the label, this new form of leadership is grounded in the theory that those closest to the scene are best able to make wise decisions about what should go on there. According to Bullard and Taylor (1993, p. 57), the factory model of hierarchical management, authoritarian teaching, and standardized learning for all is being replaced by a decentralized, shared decision-making model of teaching for learning for all in order to meet the needs both of a new age and of a multitalented, complex student population. In schools, this means that most policy and budgetary decisions about how a school will operate should be made by the local community, not by a school board or the central administration of the district. This kind of local empowerment will not be achieved without pain. Each community will have special interest groups with their own agendas, which these groups will try to impose on the schools. Whether it is advocacy for the arts or for school prayer, or opposition to sex education or to the inclusion of special education students in regular classrooms, conflict is inevitable. The Community Learning Center will have to work hard at providing opportunities for opposing views to be heard and at creating ways for developing a communitywide consensus on these and countless other issues.

Change in some school districts has been accompanied by a dramatic change in the roles of principals, teachers, parents, and community members. Cunningham and Gresso (1993, p. xi) describe the phenomenon this way: "The new paradigms of excellence recognize, develop, support, and encourage all individuals to use their knowledge, skills, and experiences to improve their organization." This means that opportunities to provide leadership must be available to people in all the stakeholder groups in the school community.

In Chapter 3, we take a closer look at the kinds of skills needed to ensure that shared decision-making works in the Community Learning Center, and at the changes in traditional roles that are required. A consequence of these changes is an evolving concept of shared ownership, in which people feel that they own not only the problems that exist in their schools, but also the processes that used to solve them. Succeeding chapters focus on important aspects of the Community Learning Center as a model for schools of the twenty-first century. While any one aspect could be implemented independently as a form of educational restructuring, readers are urged to look at the totality of what is presented, rather than the parts.

REFERENCES

Bullard, Pamela, and Barbara O. Taylor. 1933. *Making School Reform Happen*. Needham, MA: Allyn and Bacon.

Carr, William. 1942. *Community Life in a Democracy*. Chicago: National Association of Parents and Teachers.

Dewey, John. (1916). *Democracy and Education*. New York: MacMillan Company.

Decker, Larry E., and associates. 1992 (revised). *Community Education: Building Learning Communities.* Alexandria, VA: National Community Education Association.

Davies, D. 1988. "Benefits and Barriers to Parent Involvement," *Community Education Research Digest,* 2, 11–19.

Davies, D., P. Burch, and V. Johnson. 1991. *A Portrait of Schools Reaching Out.* Boston: Institute for Responsive Education.

Epstein, J. L. 1986. "Parents' Reactions to Teachers' Practices of Parent Involvement," *Elementary School Journal,* 19, 119–36.

Epstein, J. L. 1987. "Parent Involvement: What Research Says to Administrators," *Education and Urban Society,* 19, 119–36.

Epstein, J. L. 1991. "Effects on Student Achievement of Teacher Practices of Parent Involvement," in S. Sivern (ed.), *Advances in Reading/language Research, Vol. 5: Literacy Through Family, Community and School Interaction.* Greenwich, CT: JAI Press.

Everett, Samuel (ed). 1938. *The Community School.* New York: D. Appleton-Century Company.

Goodlad, John I. 1984. *A Place Called School.* New York: McGraw-Hill.

Minzey, Jack D., and Clyde E. LeTarte. 1994. *Reforming Public Schools through Community Education.* Dubuque, IA: Kendall/Hunt Publishing.

Phi Delta Kappa. 1994. *Reinventing Our Schools: A Conversation with Phillip Schlechty.* Bloomington, IN. Videotape.

Yeager, William A. 1939. *Home–School Community Relations.* Pittsburgh: University of Pittsburgh Press.

3

SHARING THE POWER

Seymour B. Sarason (1991, p. 83), writing in *The Predictable Failure of Education Reform,* highlights the frustration of being powerless:

> When one has no stake in the way things are, when one's needs or opinions are provided no forum, when one sees oneself as the object of unilateral actions, it takes no particular wisdom to suggest that one would rather be elsewhere.

The design of the Community Learning Center focuses on changing this feeling to an empowerment that allows each participant a voice in how the Center operates.

If you were to visit a Community Learning Center in a community previously served by a conventional elementary or secondary school, the first thing you would probably notice is that the learners represent a wide range of ages. Linger a while and you would observe that students and teachers are working in teams. Perhaps you would also notice that the principal—someone we are used to thinking of as the person "in charge"—is functioning more as a facilitator than a boss, and that a team of stakeholders from the community served by the school are making the decisions that were formerly made by a principal or someone from the school system's central office.

"Stakeholder" is turning up with ever greater frequency in the literature of effective organizations and successful leadership. This frustrates those of us whose electronic spell-checking programs do not recognize "stakeholder" as a word. Someone recently suggested to me that we start using the word "stockholder" instead, both because it is easily understood and because it is a sensible substitute for stakeholder.

Actually, the word "stockholder" suggests a useful analogy. The "school council" or "school improvement council" is analogous to a corporate board of directors, elected by stockholders to make decisions about how to operate the company. As in the corporate model, the school council is involved in broad-based decision-making, resource allocation, and strategic planning, but not in the micromanagement of the enterprise. School principals are still expected to provide day-to-day leadership, and teachers are still required to use their professional skills and judgment to provide instruction. Shared decision-making in the school community in no way means a diminished role for the professional educator.

A look at the membership of the teams or councils at the new Community Learning Center reveals a lot about the extent to which power and decision-making are being shared. People from these groups might serve on the council:

- Teachers (one or more from each grade level)
- Parents (one or more from each grade level)
- School support staff (a representative such as a cafeteria manager, secretary, or nurse)
- Community business managers/owners
- Human resources directors from local corporation
- Community service agencies (representatives of community health, social services, juvenile justice, and similar agencies)
- Local churches

- Service clubs (Junior League, Kiwanis, Lions, Rotary, Sertoma, etc.)
- Parent-teacher associations
- Students
- Principals

In a typical Community Learning Center, the council has 16–18 people, which is a good, workable size.

Some schools that have already moved in the direction of site-based management may have a council with membership similar to that described above, but in many schools the council is made up only of teachers and administrators. Other school councils include parents but not community members, or teachers but not students, or business people but not community service agency representatives.

There is a rationale for each category of members listed above. Teachers represent the heart and soul of a school; they are closest to the point where learning takes place and are in an excellent position to discover new ways to improve the process. Parents are good candidates for council membership because they know a lot about their own children and have a real stake in what goes on in the school. In his research for *A Place Called School*, Goodlad (1984, p. 274) found that most of the parents surveyed would "take power from the more remote, less visible, more impersonal authorities heading the system and place it in the hands of the more visible, more personally known, close-at-hand staff of the school and parent groups close to the school." Churches and service clubs can also provide a great deal of support for the work of the Community Learning Center and should be represented in the decision-making process.

The leadership of the Community Learning Center has to put in place a systematic way to encourage each segment of the community to participate in all phases of activity in the center. It is not enough just to open the front door and wait for people to join in the work and the fun. Encouragement and support must be offered to each group. Initially, this effort may take a lot of hand-holding to make sure that each targeted group feels wanted and needed, and that the center is actually serving the needs of the community.

Ironically, the students, the most important constituency of any school, comprise the group that is most often overlooked when decisions are made about a school. Sarason, in his critique of school reform efforts, *The Predictable Failure of Educational Reform* (1991, p. 113), provides a powerful argument for involving students:

> We often act as though students are the products of school, when, in fact, kids must be the workers in order to learn. They must want to come to school, and they must be willing to work, even when no one is hanging over them. If we can't achieve this, no kind of school reform, however ambitious, will improve student learning and public education. So it's hard to explain why we don't routinely ask kids—especially kids in trouble—about how to improve schools.

It should be unimaginable for a school council not to include students, especially representatives of students judged to be at risk of failure, but it is unfortunately true that genuine student involvement is not found in the decision-making process of most schools.

When it comes to selecting students to be involved in school decision-making, there is an understandable temptation to choose the student council president, the cheerleader captain, or the outstanding athlete. But when successful students are asked how a school can be improved, they typically have few ideas or suggestions; the school is obviously working just fine for them. On the other hand, students with a history of discipline problems, truancy, and poor grades may have a lot of ideas for change because the school's current programs are failing them.

The school support staff has an important role to play in establishing a good climate for learning. Office staff that doesn't treat students, teachers, and parents in a pleasant and efficient manner can set a negative tone for an entire school. A poorly run cafeteria, or a building that is not maintained with pride, can have a lot of influence on what happens in the classroom. Experience has also taught us that when members of the support staff are given an opportunity to participate, they often have creative suggestions for solving a wide range of problems faced by the school.

Although the principal is an obvious choice for membership on the school council, I have attended many school council and team meetings at which the principal either chairs the meeting or controls the agenda. It does make you wonder how much power is really being shared. The principal must be an active participant in the work of the council, but not the dominant force in its work.

Several years ago, a teacher, who was a student in one of my classes, wanted to talk about the site-based management model in use at her school. She said that the teachers and parents who were members of the school council were very excited about having a chance to be part of the decision-making process, but that they were becoming frustrated. I expected her to explain that the frustration was caused by all the time now spent in meetings, but that was not the case. She said that the council had worked hard to come up with ideas about how to improve the school, but when they took their ideas to the principal, who did not attend the meetings, he would tell them which ones they could try and which they could not. This is consistent with the view that school councils are advisory bodies without any real power or authority. This may be acceptable as a form of site-based management, but it is certainly not shared decision-making.

Jane L. David (1995, p. 4) puts the issue succinctly: "For all its guises, site-based management is basically an attempt to transform schools into communities where the appropriate people participate constructively in major decisions that affect them." This principle becomes a key element as we move to transform traditional schools into Community Learning Centers.

Shared decision-making in schools tends to fall along a continuum (see Figure 1) that starts with a traditional autocratic approach in which the principal makes decisions in isolation from the rest of the school community. As we move along the continuum, various groups are added to the process, first in an advisory capacity, then in a true sharing relationship.

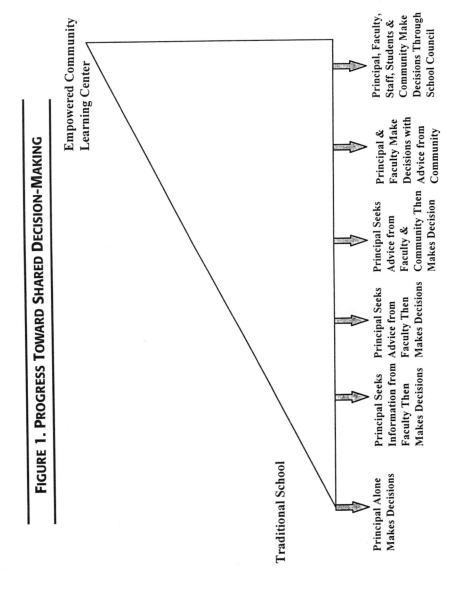

FIGURE 1. PROGRESS TOWARD SHARED DECISION-MAKING

Empowered Community Learning Center

Traditional School

Principal Alone Makes Decisions

Principal Seeks Information from Faculty Then Makes Decisions

Principal Seeks Advice from Faculty Then Makes Decisions

Principal Seeks Advice from Faculty & Community Then Makes Decision

Principal & Faculty Make Decisions with Advice from Community

Principal, Faculty, Staff, Students & Community Make Decisions Through School Council

Empowerment at the school site is founded on some basic beliefs that provide a foundation for the shared decision-making process. Those beliefs include:

+ People can be trusted to use good judgment.
+ People are more likely to change when they have a voice in making changes.
+ Those closest to the problem are in the best position to understand and solve it.
+ When people work together they lose the sense of being in separate camps.
+ The resources for change and improvement already exist in the school community.
+ Parents and community members are important contributors to the education of children.
+ Involving students in decision making gives them an opportunity to become responsible members of a democratic society.

One issue we should not try to duck when we talk about sharing power is the issue of accountability. A major problem that principals have with shared decision-making is that central administrators of school systems, after decreeing that decision-making power to is to be shared, continue to hold principals accountable for all results. Principals are saying, "This shared decision-making stuff sounds good, but when I get called into the superintendent's office for the annual review of progress at my school, comparing this year's standardized test scores to last year's, it is my butt that is on the line, not the school council's." It is hard to argue the point with these principals, but the problem lies, not in the decision-making process, but in the way people are held accountable for results.

Schools need an accountability model in which the principal is only one part of the team held responsible for the results produced by each school unit. This means that when that annual meeting is held to review each school's progress (including test scores), the principal does not go to the superintendent's office alone. The principal goes as part of the *team* that adopted the plan for producing the results under review, the plan that has been responsible for making the decisions about how teaching and learning activities are carried on, and how resources are used. This annual review should be a time for celebrating success, examining failed expectations, and planning adjustments in the school plan to improve student performance. Accountability exists only when power, and the expectation of being held accountable, are tied firmly together by a bond of mutual respect and an uncompromising commitment to improving the quality of education for every child.

COMER SCHOOLS

The Community Learning Center will adopt many of the principles that form the foundation of a school model developed by Yale University psychiatrist James Comer. He and his colleagues have been working on a design for schools that serve poor and minority children. Comer believes strongly that parents must play a major role in all aspects of the life of the school, particularly school management and governance. Comer contends that the direct involvement of parents lowers their distrust of educators. Comer schools are based on these principles:

- Schools must review problems in open discussion in a *no-fault* atmosphere.
- Each school must develop *collaborative working relationships* among principals, parents, teachers, community leaders, superintendents, and health-care workers.
- All decisions must be reached by *consensus* rather than decree. (Zimmerman, 1993, p. 17)

With students added to the list of school collaborators, Comer's principles fit comfortably into the design for the Community Learning Center. The "no-fault" atmosphere stressed by Comer is critical, because no gains will be made if every problem is approached with an attempt to place blame. Too much valuable time and energy have already been wasted in finger pointing, fruitlessly blaming each other for the failures of our schools. The Comer Schools are all participants in the School Development Project (SDP), which advocates a three-level approach that gradually moves parents from participation in social events to volunteering and, finally, into policy making (Liontos, 1992).

- ◆ Level 1. Broad-based participation.

  This level is designed to draw in most parents by offering activities that are attractive to the school community—gospel or ethnic music nights, children's pageants, or potluck dinners, for example.

- ◆ Level 2. Parent participation in day-to-day school affairs.

  At this level, parents get more involved in the life of the classrooms and the school. SDP schools don't leave this level of involvement to chance. If they find that parents are not volunteering, they conduct a recruitment program. If parents say they don't volunteer because they feel inadequate or unprepared, informal workshops are organized to discuss the skills needed and to reassure parents that sophisticated training is not needed for many school assistance tasks.

- ◆ Level 3. Parents in school governance.

  In SDP schools, parent representatives are members of the governance and management team. With emphasis on parent-staff collaboration, parents participate in the school's regular governing body rather than in a separate parent advisory group. Parents are seen as equal partners with teachers and administrators; training in participation skills is provided for all members of the governance group. "[B]y sharing in the 'ownership' of the school, parents have more of a vested interest in the outcomes of all students and are thus more willing to invest increased time and energy in maintaining trust and collaboration" (Liontos, 1992, p. 61).

Although the Comer model was developed for schools that serve disadvantaged families, I believe that its basic principles will produce gratifying results in any community.

NEW ROLES FOR SCHOOL LEADERS

As school systems begin to implement true shared decision-making, principals will need help in redefining their roles to support this new way of doing business. It should be expected that those who have power may not look favorably on giving some of it to others. This may be especially true in schools that are bringing parents and community members into the process for the first time. Teachers who have only recently acquired a share of the power themselves may, for example, be reluctant to share it further.

A good foundation for understanding the nature of this change in leadership is offered in *The Wisdom of Teams* by Katzenbach and Smith (1993, pp. 139–45). The authors identify six essential rules for effective team leadership; their recommendations are closely applicable to the emerging new roles for principals and teachers.

1. Keep the purpose, goals and approach relevant and meaningful. All teams must shape their own common purpose, performance goals, and approach.

2. Build commitment and confidence….[T]here is an important difference between individual commitment and accountability versus mutual accountability. Both are needed for any group to become a real team.

3. Strengthen the mix and level of skills….[T]he most flexible and top-performing teams consist of people with all the technical, functional, problem-solving, decision-making, interpersonal, and teamwork skills the team needs to perform. To get there, team leaders encourage people to take the risks needed for growth and development.

4. Manage relationships with outsiders, including removing obstacles. Team leaders are expected by

people outside as well as inside the team to manage much of the team's contacts and relationships with the rest of the organization.

5. Create opportunities for others....[T]he leader's challenge is to provide performance opportunities to the team and the people on it.

6. Do real work. Everyone on a real team, including the leader, does real work in roughly equivalent amounts.

Leaders in the Community Learning Center have to give their teams the kind of support outlined by Katzenbach and Smith, because the degree to which the teams function effectively directly determines the success or failure of shared decision-making.

So far I have not applied the term "empowerment" to the kind of power sharing I am advocating. Empowered people are allowed and encouraged to discover and use their own latent talents. Schools as organizations have not typically promoted individuality, creativity, or innovative thinking. According to Cunningham and Gresso (1993, p. 214), "Education is a profession of great inhibitors in a society that scorns educators' inability to respond. It is not the educators, but the disempowering culture in which they are nurtured that results in the failure to respond."

While much lip service has been paid to the decentralization of decision making and the empowerment of schools, teachers, students, parents, and community, little has actually been done to provide the tools, methods, and skills that could help the empowered make intelligent choices about how to improve the performance of their schools. Many school systems fear that decentralized decision-making by the newly empowered will lead to unfortunate or, at best, uncoordinated decision making. Some will try empowerment for a time and then abandon empowerment as a bad idea, when it may have been the right idea but it lacked the kind of support it needed to succeed.

The Community Learning Center, instead of being a place in which people must turn to others for approval, or must follow tightly prescribed rules, is a place in which people are expected to act responsibly, and to be concerned with the consequences of their actions. Empowerment in this new culture must take place in two dimensions. First, individuals must develop a sense of personal self-confidence; the external support of the old culture must give way to self-support of the individual. Second, the new culture must support group understanding and the capability of the group to take effective action.

To be successful in this new culture, the Community Learning Center has to give members of the school community the skills and knowledge necessary to make empowered shared decision-making work. As a result of my work with school councils and teams in recent years, I have identified a number of skill areas that are important to the success of an empowered culture. I call these skill areas Team Process Skills:

- Synergism: The Real Power of Teams
- Developing a Shared Vision
- Team Problem Solving
- Team Decision Making
- Conflict Management
- Strategic Planning
- Meeting Management
- Leadership Development

Each of these areas represents specific knowledge, skills and experience that can be shared with others in the community. Without a foundation of skills in these areas, people who are expected to exercise individual and group power may flounder and fail to reach an effective level of performance, not because they lack ability, but because they have not been given the tools to be successful. The process of changing the culture of schools is not complete until everyone has had the opportunity to develop the skills required in this new environment.

In every community, lines need to be drawn between those decisions that will be delegated to individual schools and those that will be made by administrative staff or the school board. Decisions that have usually been shared with local schools are:

- Needs Assessment
- Goal Setting
- Program Development
- Scheduling
- Allocating Resources*
- Hiring and Assigning Staff*
- Staff Development Program*
- Evaluating Results

The three areas that are most likely to be met with resistance in any decentralization effort are marked with an asterisk. While it is true that some resource allocation decisions have been made by individual schools, those decisions are often mere tokens, which do not involve major changes in the way that the school operates. In the case of hiring and staffing decisions, most are fully controlled by the central office staff. Similarly, decisions about staff development programs are not ordinarily made at the level of the individual school. Unfortunately, this may be one of the most serious limitations on local school control, because intensive staff development is often needed to support school-site initiatives. Moreover, Sirotnik and Goodlad (1988) and others have found that site-based staff development is more effective as part of school renewal or restructuring efforts than is systemwide staff development.

Certain decisions cannot be delegated by the school board to individual school councils because of limitations established by state law and regulations governing the operation of public schools. A recent departure from the traditional pattern of school board control is the emergence of charter schools.

CHARTER SCHOOLS

In a sense, charter schools represent the ultimate in site-based decision-making. More than a dozen states have already adopted legislation allowing a group of community members, parents, or teachers—or a combination of the three —to petition the local school board to establish an independently operated school in the community. In general, charter schools must be open to the public and they are eligible to receive state and local support roughly equal to the amount that is currently spent per pupil in the chartering district. Many states allow charter schools to seek waivers from various state requirements imposed on other public schools.

The whole concept of charter schools is not without controversy. Their plans raise a number of issues that are highly volatile in many communities, including:

- A potential for diluting the support base of other public schools.
- The possibility of opening the door to the establishment of tax-supported religious schools.
- Neglect of services to special-needs children who may be denied admission to a charter school.
- A diminished role for the professional educator in the design and provision of education programs.
- Loss of control over the quality of education and other effects that may result from the waiver of various state requirements.

Charter schools rouse mixed feelings in many public school supporters. Wilt (1994, p. 18), writing in a special issue of the *Community Education Journal* devoted to the subject of school-based decision-making, points out that "[a]t the heart of the charter school movement is the motivation to make decision making inclusive rather than exclusive. Community educators have long been advocates of this way of doing business." At this point, with few charter schools up and running, it is too early to tell what the end result of the charter school movement will be. It may be that a well-conceived system of school-based decision-making offers the best current alternative to the charter school option as a way to provide an inclusive process.

The school council cannot be the sole means for involving all of the school community's "stockholders" in the Community Learning Center. In fact, I have worked with school communities where the school council was part of the problem, rather than part of the solution.

One school had had a school council in place for two or three years. Members of the council were beginning to function effectively as a team, but a rift had developed between the council and the other school constituents—teachers, parents, and community members—who were not members of the council. It seems that council members had been focusing so intently on sharpening their own decision-making and problem-solving skills, that they had become isolated from those who they were supposed to be representing. Teachers who were not members of the council complained that they never knew what the council was going to do next; they would see new policies and programs put in place without much knowledge of where these policies and programs had come from. When they would ask about these changes, the principal would tell them it was the council that had taken the action. The teachers said that they rarely knew what was going to be on the council's agenda, and they did not feel comfortable attending council meetings to express their opinions on issues. They felt that if they raised questions about the council they would be seen as not being supportive of the school-based management system the school district was trying to put in place.

Every school council should consider establishing a plan to increase the active participation of various key groups outside the membership of the council. This could be done by setting up committees or task forces that could extend the work of the council. Specialized committees might focus on:

- ◆ Family involvement
- ◆ Improvement of reading instruction
- ◆ Community partnerships
- ◆ School volunteers
- ◆ An annual school plan
- ◆ Buildings and grounds improvement

Each group would receive direction from the school council but would be free to adopt its own agenda and work plan. Reports and recommendations for action would be presented to the council for action. These groups can be very productive and can actually take on a good part of the work that needs to be done in the ongoing task of improving the quality of education. Sharing the work with a wider group in the school community lightens the load of the school council and allows it to spend more time on the central issue of strategic planning.

Besides increasing the number of people actively involved in the work of improving the school, committees and task forces can serve as leadership development tools. People who have gained experience in one group can move on to provide leadership in another area. Figure 2 suggests the dynamics of this kind of leadership development.

A central purpose of sharing power is, of course, the development of a broad sense of ownership in the enterprise of public education. For too long we have tolerated the large numbers of community members who have no sense of involvement or ownership in local schools. Widening the circle of involvement in decisions about what the schools should be doing for the community's children, youth, and adults is an effective way to build a sense of ownership and community.

TIME

Time is a critical resource in the sharing of power. Researchers studying site-based management found that there is often too little time available for the meetings that are necessary if shared decision-making is to be truly inclusive (Mohrman and Wohlstetter, 1994).

The scheduling of meetings is another critical time issue. Leonard (1997) found that even those who talk about the need to increase parent involvement, faced with the option of holding evening meetings to allow working parents to attend, chose to continue to meet in the afternoon. The Community Learning Center has to find creative ways to provide all of the stakeholders with time to participate.

FIGURE 2. WIDENING THE CIRCLE OF INVOLVEMENT

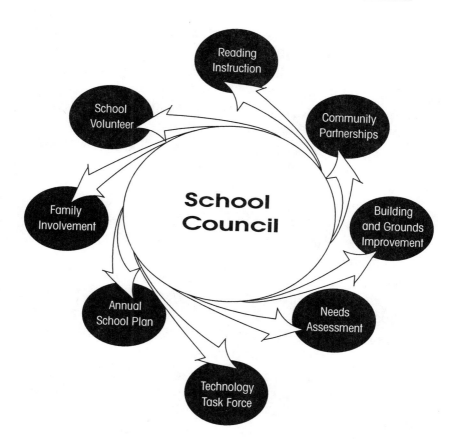

REFERENCES

Cunningham, William G., and Don W. Gresso. 1993. *Cultural Leadership: The Culture of Excellence in Education.* Needingham Heights, MA.

David, J. L. 1996. "The Who, What and Why of Site-Based Management," *Educational Leadership*, 53, 4.

Katzenbach, Jon R., and Douglas K. Smith. 1993. *The Wisdom of Teams.* New York: Harper-Collins.

Leonard, R. 1997. *A Case Study of the Action Research Process in a School for At-Risk Students.* Unpublished dissertation. Blacksburg, VA: Virginia Polytechnic Institute and State University.

Liontos, Lynn B. 1992. *At-Risk Families and Schools Becoming Partners.* Eugene, OR: ERIC Clearinghouse on Educational Management.

Mohrman, S. A., and P. Wohlstetter. 1994. *School-Based Management: Organizing for High Performance.* San Francisco: Jossey-Bass.

Sarason, Seymour B. 1991. *The Predictable Failure of Educational Reform.* San Francisco: Jossey-Bass.

Sirotnik, Kenneth A., and John I. Goodlad. 1988. *School–University Partnerships in Action.* New York: Teachers College Press.

Wilt, Joan. 1994. "Charter Schools: Opportunities for Community Education," *Community Education Journal*, XXI, 2.

Zimmerman, J. 1993. "The Comer School Development Program," *Education Research Consumer Guide Number 6.* Washington, DC: U.S. Department of Education, OERI.

4

PARTNERSHIPS WITH FAMILIES

Parents, families, and community are as much a part of the Community Learning Center as the roof, the walls, and the doors. As much care and investment must be directed to developing partnerships with families and the community as are put into the planning of the building itself.

THE FAMILY

The recent shift from a focus on involving parents to a focus on involving families in the education of children may seem to some a minor distinction, but it is an important one for many children. For some children, the primary caregiver is an aunt, an uncle, a grandparent, or even an older sibling. Linda Moore (1993, p. 31) offers a new definition of what constitutes a family:

> The United States is expanding its definition of "family." Gone are the days when "family" consisted of Mom, Dad, Dick, Jane, Puff, and Spot. "Family" now includes single mothers and children, single fathers and children, grandparents

raising children, single unrelated adults living together and, increasingly, single adults living alone
who claim other "family" members living elsewhere.

This change in definition requires that we also change the
way we think about our students' support systems. The
Community Learning Center develops strategies to establish
strong partnerships with students' families, however families are defined. This chapter offers a guide for the development of family partnerships in the Community Learning
Center.

BARRIERS TO FAMILY INVOLVEMENT

In a review of the research base for family involvement in
learning, the U.S. Department of Education (1994) addressed
the central question of why, if family involvement is so important, more of it isn't happening. The department identified four aspects of modern living that interfere with
involvement.

- **Time.**

  A study by the Families and Work Institute (1994)
  reported that 66 percent of employed parents
  with children under 18 say they do not have
  enough time for their children. Teachers, too, say
  they do not have time to make home visits or to
  meet with parents in addition to conducting their
  regular classroom activities.

- **Uncertainty about what to do.**

  Many parents are unsure how to help their children learn (National Commission on Children,
  1991). The schools themselves have not done a
  good job of preparing students—especially teenagers—for parenthood. Parents say they would
  be willing to work more with their children if
  teachers would give them more guidance (Epstein, 1987; Henderson, Marburger, and Ooms,
  1986). Teacher education programs must share

some of the blame for not adequately preparing teachers to work effectively with parents. While some state education departments acknowledge the importance of working with families, few require extensive preservice or inservice training in parent involvement (Radcliff, Malone, and Nathan, 1994).

♦ **Cultural barriers.**

Language barriers are a special problem for some families in our culturally diverse population. Teachers who are unable to communicate with non-English-speaking parents have difficulty in obtaining the kind of support many children need to be successful in the classroom. There are also many differences in the way parents with different cultural backgrounds view the schools, teaching, and their own role in their children's education (Comer, 1988; Moles, 1993).

♦ **Lack of a supportive environment.**

The level of support given by the family may be influenced by the family's economic condition. More children than at any time since 1965 live in poverty (Childrens Defense Fund, 1994), and low-income parents have been found to have less contact with schools than their better-off counterparts (Moles, 1993). Schools cannot ignore these facts. They must reach out to all parents on a continuing basis, using a wide variety of approaches.

The Community Learning Center, as examples later in this chapter show, uses its resources to build the kind of partnership with a family that is needed to assure that every child is successful.

WHAT OTHER EVIDENCE SUPPORTS FAMILY INVOLVEMENT?

Anne Henderson (1981, 1987, 1994) has summarized research showing the positive effect of family and parent involvement on the education of children in a series of publications that have come to be known as the Evidence Series. In the most recent edition, she writes, "Now, in 1994, the field [of family involvement] has become a growth industry. We found more studies than we could possibly include" (1994, p. ix). Based on their research, Henderson and her associates have issued powerful statements about the value of family and parent involvement.

> The evidence is now *beyond dispute* [emphasis added]. When schools work together with families to support learning, children tend to succeed not just in school, but throughout life. In fact, the most accurate predictor of a student's achievement in school is not income or social status, but the extent to which that student's family is able to:
>
> 1. Create a home environment that encourages learning.
> 2. Express high (but not unrealistic) expectations for their children's achievement and future careers.
> 3. Become involved in their children's education at the school and in the community.
>
> Taken together, the studies summarized in this report strongly suggest that when schools support families to develop these three conditions, children from low-income families and diverse cultural backgrounds approach the grades and test scores expected for middle-class children. (Henderson and Berla, 1994, p. 1)

The major themes that emerge again and again from the studies reviewed by Henderson and Berla (1994, pp. 4–5) include:

- ♦ The family makes critical contributions to student achievement, from earliest childhood through high school. Efforts to improve children's outcomes are much more effective if they encompass their families.

- When parents are involved at school, not just at home, children do better in school, and they stay in school longer.

- When parents are involved at school, their children go to a better school.

- Children do best when their parents are enabled to play four key roles in their children's learning: as teachers, supporters, advocates, and decision-makers.

- The more the relationship between family and school approaches a comprehensive, well-planned partnership, the higher the student's achievement.

- Families, schools, and community organizations all contribute to student achievement and the best results come when all three work together.

STRATEGIES FOR ACTION

How to involve families and parents in their children's education is a primary concern in the design of the new Community Learning Center. The research has given us a clear idea of some of the things we will *not* do:

- We will not underestimate the power of strong family and parent involvement.

- We will not wait until the children formally register as students to get families involved in their educational development.

- We will not depend on single-track strategies to provide the kind of involvement that will have a positive effect on student achievement.

- We will not expect all parents and families to become involved in the same way.

- We will not assume that low-income families are unable or unwilling to become involved in their children's education.

Still, the hard question remains: How will we make strong, positive connections with families and parents? In *The Basic School: A Community for Learners*, Ernest Boyer (1995, p. 47) makes a persuasive case for beginning to make partnerships with parents in the preschool years:

> In the Basic School, the circle of community extends outward to embrace parents, who are viewed as the child's first and most important teachers. A vital partnership is created between the home and school, one that begins during the preschool years, is strengthened when the child formally enrolls, and continues from kindergarten through grade five.

The Basic School proposed by Boyer has many similarities to the Community Learning Center.

PRESCHOOL PROGRAMS

We cannot wait until parents bring their children to kindergarten. Goal 1 of the Goals 2000: Educate America Act is that all children will start school ready to learn. Obviously, this goal will not become a reality unless we reach out to parents before their children reach school age.

One effective way to get families involved is to send representatives of the school into the community to visit parents in their homes. A program with the unlikely name of HIPPY (Home Instruction Program for Preschool Youngsters) has a two-year curriculum that prepares the mothers of four- and five-year-old children to teach skills that will increase readiness for kindergarten. Founded in Israel to help disadvantaged children, HIPPY has been making slow headway in the United States since its introduction in 1984 (Liontos, 1992). Parent aides, hired from the local community, conduct the instruction. During home visits and group meetings, the parent aides role-play, using the educational materials with the parents. The home visits are scheduled during both daytime and evening hours to accommodate working parents. Parent participants receive materials to use in working at home with the children for 15–20 minutes each day.

In Arkansas, the HIPPY program has received state support for implementation in every community. The Arkansas Department of Education (1991, p. 6) has adopted these objectives:

1. Provide instruction for four- and five-year-olds to ensure preparation for learning in kindergarten.
2. Involve the mother or parent in the role of educator for her child.
3. Provide motivating activities for parent awareness of education and vocational opportunities.
4. Provide parents with information on resources in the community that can meet their various needs.
5. Provide parents with an opportunity to increase their skills to be more effective parents.
6. Provide parents with motivation to become involved in the activities in the public schools.

An evaluation of Arkansas' HIPPY program concluded: "The outcome of the performance level of HIPPY children in the public schools has proven the program's success. The attitude of HIPPY parents toward their child's education has had a tremendously positive outcome as well." (Arkansas Department of Education 1991, p. 9)

In Darlington County, South Carolina, an early education program called Catch 'Em in the Cradle is built on the belief that a child's first and most important teachers are the child's parents, and that children learn best through active parental participation (Byrd 1994).

The Norfolk, Virginia, school district employs local parents as "parent involvement technicians" in each of its 50 schools. Parents from the community often have an easier time than school personnel in gaining acceptance by other parents and having access to their homes. After completing a well-designed training program, parents have proven to be very effective. A similar program, Parents As Teachers, is operated statewide in Missouri.

Community Learning Centers that serve the lower grade levels have an Office of Early Childhood Development headed by a staff that has professional preparation in the field of early childhood development. This office works with the community to plan and conduct programs designed to support families to assure that every child is ready to learn when the child enters the formal instructional program of the Center.

The parent involvement program in the Community Learning Center has these features:

- ◆ Parents from the community act as outreach technicians to work with parents and families in the community.

- ◆ A parent educator is employed to facilitate the design and implementation of programs to help parents improve their parenting skills. (This educator also works with the parents of older students in the community).

- ◆ A developmental daycare center provides both pre-school education and after-school programs for enrolled students who need additional support to reap full benefit from the center's regular instructional program.

PARENT EDUCATION PROGRAMS

Some parent education programs focus on pre- school parents, while others are developed for the parents of school-aged children. Some parent education programs have been poorly attended in the past because many parents believed that attendance was an admission that they were bad parents.

Today, many communities have been able to turn around this negative public perception of parent education. Parents in these communities now understand that most of us have never received help in learning how to be good parents. Someone recently observed that a child is the only thing in every household that comes without an instruction manual. We have instructions on how to program the VCR, how to use the microwave oven, and how to maintain the car. But little help has been available on how to do a better job of raising our children.

Community Learning Center parent education programs are not developed solely by staff, but are planned with the full involvement of the parents themselves. All applicable resources in the community are brought together to provide effective parent education. Among those groups providing assistance are community mental health agencies, youth organizations (Boy and Girl Scouts, the Y's, 4-H, etc.), the Cooperative Extension Service, and healthcare agencies. The parent educator employed by the Community Learning Center facilitates the development of the program, but the actual planning and instruction is done jointly by resource organizations from the community. Parent education programs are offered in the Center itself and in other community venues in order to assure the widest possible access.

Fathers are also involved in the development of parent education programs, sharing responsibility for raising children to be successful in life. Programs like the Father Reengagement Initiative operated by the Philadelphia Children's Network will be developed; this program helps men engage in activities with their children in order to increase fathers' emotional and financial support for their kids. Studies have found that even in two-parent families, mothers are more active in school events than fathers (Center for Workforce Preparation, 1994). The Community Learning Center develops strategies to reverse this trend.

A PARENT RESOURCE CENTER

The Community Learning Center has a Parent Resource Center (PRC)—a place for parents to go when they come into the building. PRC staff and volunteers will provide an atmosphere designed to make parents feel comfortable and welcome. A wide variety of parenting resources and guides will be available, including materials (math manipulatives, books, videotapes, etc.) that can be taken home to use with children. A computer is available to provide access to the Internet, so parents are able to find valuable information such as that provided by the National Parent Information Network (NPIN) sponsored by the ERIC Clearinghouse on Elementary and Secondary Education. (See Appendix A for a listing of resources.) Parents are also able to log on to the

Community Learning Center's local area network and leave electronic messages for their children and their children's teachers, or check on a child's academic progress. Information about school activities and community services is provided on the computer in the Parent Resource Center.

Some schools are already using their voice mail messaging systems to tell callers what is happening in individual classrooms on any given day; parents can call a dedicated phone line and enter the voice mailbox for their child's class. Teachers can update messages daily, describing specific skills being worked on, homework assignments, and even lists of items needed for class. At the end of the recorded message, parents and student callers may leave their own messages. Parents may provide feedback about their children's classroom experiences. Many parents express appreciation to the teacher or leave other messages of support.

PARENT-TEACHER CONFERENCES

Almost anyone, parent or teacher, who has participated in the rite of the parent-teacher conference will tell you that the conference is not something that they look forward to with great enthusiasm. If we were all completely honest, we would probably admit that most of us view these semiannual events as painful and not particularly helpful. Parents often report that they don't gain insight into their children's education from the conferences, and teachers frequently complain that they rarely get to talk with the parents of the students who are most in need of help. Still, the parent-teacher conference does reinforce the idea that parents and teachers can work together as a team.

The Community Learning Center adds an important stakeholder to the parent-teacher conference—the student. Parents will be asked to sign a contract when their children enroll in the Community Learning Center; the contract will, among other things, ask both parent and child to agree to participate in every conference, at which parents, teachers, and student will meet around a table where the student's portfolio of work will be presented. The parents will meet with all of the student's teachers as a team, so that the total development of the student can be viewed. This will contrast with the segmented view parents have received in the past, when they met separately with each subject-matter teacher. Students are involved in developing a specific plan for improvements that need to be made in the coming months, so they can begin to assume more responsibility for their own learning. (A more detailed discussion of the portfolio approach to student assessment is provided in Chapter 5.)

PARENT-TEACHER RESEARCH

The Schools Reaching Out (SRO) project directed by Don Davies and associates at Boston University provides a model of parent-teacher collaboration centered around action research teams that involve teachers and parents in the development of action plans for improving their own school. A researcher/facilitator guides the process at each school. Parents and teachers are invited to meet to learn more about action research, and a group is formed to undertake an action research project that is aimed at school improvement. The group identifies research topics based on the group's interests and on data collected about conditions in the school. Among the topics that the SRO groups identified for study were ways to improve student attendance, ways to raise scores on standardized math tests, and strategies for getting more parents of at-risk students involved in the school.

Burch (1993, p. 16), writing about the action research projects, concluded that "...although parent-teacher action research is not a cure-all, the person-to-person affirmation and challenges of collaboration invite change in vision and action. Parent-teacher action researchers can be an integral part of a school's transformation."

FAMILY FRIENDLY EMPLOYERS

Members of the corporate community are beginning to recognize that, as a nation, we will never meet the goal of having children enter school ready to learn, unless business leaders become involved. Businesses can do some specific things to support the involvement of families in children's education (U.S. Department of Education, 1995):

♦ Provide flextime and leave policies that make it possible for parents to visit schools during the day.

♦ Support parent education programs, perhaps held at the parent's work site during lunch periods or downtime.

♦ Improve child care to eliminate the unevenness of availability of quality care.

Thirteen percent of the nation's larger employers already provide child care at on-site or near-site centers, and educational participation days, which gives all employees paid leave for the purpose of participating in school activities. Robert Allen, chief executive officer of AT&T, says:

> We have not traditionally linked the well-being of children to the success of business or the governance of nations. Yet increasingly we're acknowledging that upheavals in the American family aren't self-contained—they intersect with business and economic circles and loop into the social fabric of this nation. As a society, we assume a larger affiliation—one that implies, not just family ties, but added obligations. (U.S. Department of Education 1995, p. 3)

BREAKING THE CURVE

A downward curve in the level of family involvement is clearly observable after the elementary school years. A study by Child Trends, Inc., found that nearly 50 percent of high school students have parents who do not volunteer at school and do not attend PTA meetings, back-to-school nights, class plays, or athletic events (*Virginia Pilot*, 1994). The study found that the level of involvement falls from 73 percent for the parents of children aged 8 to 11 to 50 percent for the parents of children 16 and older. Another interesting finding of the Child Trend study was that mothers who worked outside the home were just as involved as those who did not.

The Community Learning Centers serving high school students will have to place far greater emphasis on building and strengthening family partnerships than high schools have in the past. Currently, high levels of involvement are characteristic of parents who focus on narrow interests—band boosters and athletic clubs, for instance. These narrowly focused groups tend to involve too few parents and rarely address the broad issues of student achievement.

The Parent Teachers Association (PTA) may be the right vehicle for building support for family partnerships, but there may be a need to develop additional avenues for reaching parents. Key parent and community leaders need to be recruited to assist in efforts to build family partnerships at the secondary level. The fact that the school has reinvented itself as a Community Learning Center will provide a great deal of overall support to the notion of involving families in their children's education at all grade levels.

COMMITTING RESOURCES TO FAMILY INVOLVEMENT

On numerous occasions I have talked with educators about involving parents and families in their children's education, often sharing research that demonstrates a strong relationship between family involvement and academic achievement. The response I get is almost always positive. Yes, these educators tell me, we have seen the literature and have read those research studies. When I pursue the subject with a direct question—How are you doing in getting parents and families involved in your schools?—the answer I get, more often than not, is that it is really hard in today's world to get busy parents involved.

Then I come to the hard question: What resources are your schools committing to making things happen in the area of family and parent involvement? Educators will argue that everyone in the school is committed to getting families involved; it is even a goal in our annual school improvement plan, they will say. But it is often true that everyone's job is nobody's job. Unless the school staff is committed to providing ongoing leadership to a comprehensive parent involvement plan, it usually does not happen. Resources for schools are scarce in most communities, but some resources simply must be allocated to support family and parent involvement. This allocation should be viewed as an investment that will yield a return of increased community support for the educational program of the school and improved academic achievement by students.

THE NATIONAL PARTNERSHIP

Early in 1995, a group of people representing some of the most important organizations in the country came together to adopt a strategic plan for developing a new Family Involvement Partnership for Learning to promote greater family involvement in children's learning through the development of family-school-community partnerships. The driving force behind this effort came from the National Council for Parent Involvement in Education (NCPIE) and the U.S. Department of Education.

The initial partnership affiliates included more than 100 organizations, such as the National PTA, the U.S. Chamber of Commerce Center for Workforce Preparation, the National Community Education Association, the National Association of Partners in Education, the National Associations of Elementary and Secondary Principals, the Association for Supervision and Curriculum Development, the National Alliance of Business, and the National Council of Churches, to name just a few. The partnership's mission is described in the strategic plan adopted to direct the work of the partnership:

> The American family is the bedrock on which a strong education foundation must be built to prepare our children for the rigors of the 21st Century. This Partnership seeks to launch a grassroots movement across this country—including all families, whether they are rich or poor or well-educated or less educated; and all communities, whether urban, suburban or rural—to promote and support family involvement for learning. (National Family Involvement Partnership for Learning, 1995, p. 1)

MEASURING FAMILY INVOLVEMENT

Few schools have developed a way to measure the effectiveness of their efforts to involve parents and families in children's education. But if we do not measure the results of partnerships with families and communities, we won't be able to strengthen those things that are working and rethink those that are not. The Community Learning Center will have to develop reliable indicators and measuring techniques for assessing progress toward greater family involvement in the learning of children and youth. Accurate and cost-effective indicators and measuring instruments are needed to determine the extent and quality of:

- Family involvement in the school.
- Family involvement with students in carrying out learning activities in the home.
- Success in family-school-community-business partnerships.
- Involvement of families and parents previously considered hard to reach.

Self-evaluation instruments will also be needed, so that families, schools, and communities can assess their own efforts in support of family involvement in children's education. It is only through the collection of such data that we will be able to tell whether we are making any progress.

PARTNERSHIP DEVELOPMENT

The Community Learning Center serves as the hub of partnerships between the home, school, and community. The development of partnerships needs the support and nurturing of the staff of the Community Learning Center in collaboration with community leaders. There are many solid reasons for schools to assume the leadership role in developing home-school collaboration:

- Parental involvement has been shown to have a positive and significant effect on student achievement. Collaboration with parents would greatly enhance the mission and work of the school.

- No other agency or organization has proven ready, willing, and capable of being effective in building true collaboration with parents and schools.

- Schools hold a position of respect in most communities.

- Many parents simple do not know what to do to help their children or how to do it. Schools can provide parents with the knowledge and skills that they need to be good teachers of their own children.

- The school is responsible for the barriers that inhibit parental participation in school; only the school can tear down those barriers.

Epstein (1995) developed a taxonomy for describing various types of parental participation that improve students' achievement. Her six types of involvement are used as a foundation to establish family partnerships in the Community Learning Center. Parents and families will be encouraged to carry out these roles:

- Parenting: providing for the basic physical and psychological needs of children before they leave for school.

- Communicating: responding to communications from the school.

- Volunteering: participating actively in the activities and programs of the Community Learning Center.

- Learning at Home: participating in learning activities in the home with the child.

- Decision making: participating in decisions involving the operation and programs of the Community Learning Center.

+ Collaborating with the Community: becoming advocates for the cooperative delivery of services in the community.

No other activity of the Community Learning Center will has a higher priority than the development and support of family partnerships. This commitment will be reflected in all aspects of the Community Learning Center programs.

REFERENCES

Arkansas Department of Education. 1991. *Home Instruction Program for Preschool Youngsters: Final Report.* Little Rock, AK.

Boyer, E. L. 1995. *The Basic School: A Community for Learning.* Princeton, NJ: Carnegie Foundation for the Advancement of Teaching.

Byrd, Mary A. Undated. "Catch'em in the Cradle," in *Parent Involvement (Profiles in Action Series).* Ellenton, FL: Info-Media, Inc.

Burch, P. 1993. "Circles of Change: Action Research in Family-School-Community Partnerships," *Equity and Choice,* 10, 1 (fall).

Center for Workforce Preparation. 1994. *On Target: Effective Parent Involvement Programs.* Washington, DC.

Children's Defense Fund. 1994. *The State of America's Children (Yearbook).* Washington, DC.

Comer, J. P. 1988. "Educating Poor Minority Children," *Scientific American,* 259(5), 42–48.

Epstein, J. L. 1987. "Parent Involvement: What Research Says to Administrators," *Education and Urban Society,* 19, 119–36 (February).

Epstein, J. L. 1988. "How Do We Improve Programs for Parent Involvement?," *Educational Horizons,* 66, 58–59.

Epstein, J. L. 1995. "School/Family/Community Partnerships: Caring for the Children We Share," *Kappan,* May 1995, 701–12.

Families and Work Institute. 1994. *Employers, Families and Education: Facilitating Family Involvement in Learning.* New York.

Henderson, A. T. 1981. *Parent Participation—Student Achievement: The Evidence Grows.* Columbia, MD: National Committee for Citizens in Education.

Henderson, A. T. 1987. *The Evidence Continues to Grow: Parent Involvement Improves Student Achievement. An Annotated Bibliography.* Columbia, MD: National Committee for Citizens in Education.

Henderson, A. T., and N. Berla. 1994. *A New Generation of Evidence: The Family Is Critical to Student Achievement.* Washington, DC: National Committee for Citizens in Education.

Henderson, A. T., C. L. Marburger, and T. Ooms. 1986. *Beyond the Bake Sale: An Educator's Guide to Working With Parents.* Columbia, MD: National Committee for Citizens in Education.

Liontos, Lynn B. 1992. *At-Risk Families and Schools Becoming Partners.* Eugene, OR: ERIC Clearinghouse on Educational Management.

Moles, O. C. 1993. "Collaboration Between Schools and Disadvantaged Parents: Obstacles and Openings," in N. Chavkin, ed., *Families and Schools in a Pluralistic Society.* Albany, NY: State University of New York Press.

Moore, Linda. 1993. "Re-defining, Re-inventing, and Re-establishing Community," in S. Thompson, ed., *Whole Child—Whole Community.* Boston: Institute for Responsive Education.

National Commission on Children. (1991). *Speaking of Kids: A National Survey of Children and Parents.* Washington, DC.

National Family Involvement Partnership for Learning. 1995. *National Family Involvement Partnership for Learning Strategic Plan.* Washington, DC.

Radcliff, B., M. Malone, and J. Nathan. 1994. *Training for Parent Partnership: Much More Should Be Done.* Minneapolis:

University of Minnesota, Hubert H. Humphrey Institute of Public Affairs, Center for School Change.

U.S. Department of Education. 1994. *Strong Families, Strong Schools: Building Community Partnerships for Learning.* Washington, DC.

U.S. Department of Education. 1995. *Employers, Families, and Education.* Washington, DC.

Virginia Pilot. 1994. "Parents Less Involved in Kids' High Schools," quoted in *New York Times,* September 5, 1994, p. 14.

5

TEACHING
AND LEARNING
WITH THE COMMUNITY

The Community Learning Center is a genuine learning community. Four basic principles govern the Center and its classrooms. First, learning extends beyond the classroom to include all the resources of the community. Second, teachers are facilitators of learning rather than dispensers of knowledge. Third, students are expected to be active learners, taking part in the work of developing a context for their own learning. Fourth, every student has the support of a mentor from the community who takes an active interest in the student's intellectual and social development.

This chapter explores the notion of a curriculum in which resources from the community are integrated into the teaching and learning processes. We also examine some different ways in which teachers and students can work together in collaborative relationships.

TEACHERS

A group of teachers met in Snowbird, Utah, in 1989, to develop a vision of the future of American education. They defined educators in a way that fits very well into the framework of the Community Learning Center.

> Educators are the professional teachers in the community—the specialists who have specifically learned how people learn, how to motivate people, how to organize instruction, and how individuals grow and develop. They guide the learner's relationship with the larger community. (Impact II, 1991, p. 11)

The Teachers Network, as the group came to be known, pointed out that teachers need a knowledge of child development, learning theory, teaching modalities, and curriculum development. But they noted that future teachers will also have to focus on family and community leadership theory, problem solving and conflict resolution, and teacher evaluation. The Impact II teachers said that because future teachers will also be involved in school decision-making, they will need courses in budgeting, finance, and management.

This description of teachers provides a good foundation for building the faculty of the Community Learning Center. Teachers play a central role in developing the curriculum, selecting resources and deciding how to use them, and choosing the means and methods that will be used to help students learn. Terms like "choreographer," "facilitator," and "encourager of the learning process" accurately describe the function of teachers in the Center.

The staffing model developed by Designs for Learning (1995, p. 6) in its Community Learning Centers project offers a guide:

> Staffing is based on elevating the position of teachers to "facilitators of learning." Teacher productivity is increased with the assistance of paraprofessionals, clerks, technology specialists, community resource linkers and volunteers. Levels of teaching are compensated on the basis of responsibility,

skill, productivity and other factors. Staffing includes others: parents, community resource people (citizens, seniors, business employees, agency staff) and students.

The teacher in the Community Learning Center will be a collaborator—a team leader and guide, rather than a boss. The teacher will model values that encourage students to be committed to inquiry, collaborative effort, and lifelong learning.

Community educators have a motto: "Everyone a learner, everyone a teacher." Teaching in the Community Learning Center becomes a shared function. Not only do teachers learn from each other how to improve their practice, but students serve as teachers, sharing what they have learned with other students. Teachers are often found among community members who have talents and skills to share in the school community. There is a strong commitment to support the role of parents as the child's first teachers. As Ernest Boyer (1995) puts it, the teacher will be a leader and the parents will be partners.

THE CLASSROOMS

The classrooms of the Community Learning Center are learner-centered. Students are encouraged to take responsibility for their own learning, becoming active learners rather than passive processors of information.

John Dewey (1900) wrote of his frustration in trying to buy suitable desks and chairs for students. After he had experienced considerable difficulty in finding what he was looking for, he encountered one dealer, "more intelligent than the rest," who remarked, "I am afraid we have not what you want. You want something at which the children may work; these are all for listening." Dewey commented:

> That tells the story of the traditional education. Just as the biologist can take a bone or two and reconstruct the whole animal, so, if we put before the mind's eye the ordinary schoolroom, with its rows of ugly desks placed in geometrical order, crowded together so that there shall be as little moving room

as possible, desks almost all of the same size, with just space enough to hold book, pencils, and paper, and add a table, some chairs, the bare walls, and possibly a few pictures, we can reconstruct the only educational activity that can possibly go on in such a place. It is all made for listening. (p. 50)

If we take Dewey's message to heart, we will not design classrooms around the notion of students as listeners. Classrooms in the Community Learning Center will have furniture flexible enough to be arranged in large- and small-group configurations that will allow students the kind of space they to need to be active learners.

STUDENTS

Because students are expected to take responsibility for their own learning, teachers must create an environment that will allow them to assume that responsibility. As Brooks and Brooks (1993, p. 49) explain: "Teachers do this by encouraging self-initiated inquiry, providing the materials and supplies appropriate for the learning tasks, and sensitively mediating teacher/student and student/student interactions." They emphasize that teachers should not take sole responsibility for their students' learning.

Once the student's role in the learning process is clearly understood, the issue of how to organize students for instruction must be addressed. The practice of "tracking"—that is, grouping students according to their ability—has dominated the landscape of schools for most of the past two decades. We have become so accepting of tracking as a way of organizing our schools that we seldom question the practice. Bullard and Taylor (1993, p. 20) discuss the rationale:

> The reasoning behind tracking is that by putting students into groups according to what someone perceives as their ability, schools are able to cater to specific achievement levels, thus making teaching more efficient. It is also argued that tracking prevents psychological damage to lower-level students who would be competing with the higher achievers. Also, tracking is supposed to make the

teaching task simpler; teachers can manage students more easily.

Bullard and Taylor cite the work of Jeannie Oakes, an authority on tracking, to support their conclusion that there is little evidence to support the widespread use of tracking. Research shows that not only are students in the lower tracks adversely affected, but students in the top tracks do not have their learning enhanced. Critics of tracking also point to the inequity that results when a majority of lower-track students are of one race and social class. In these cases, all students are denied the opportunity to learn how to interact with people who are different from themselves.

In practice, tracking becomes a vicious circle. A student is placed in a lower track because someone thinks that is where the student belongs. Teachers who work with low-track groups have been found to have low expectations of them. So, because little is expected, these students may produce at levels lower than they are capable of, reinforcing their placement in the low track. Once a student is labeled low-track, or nonacademic, it is difficult or impossible for that student to move to a higher level.

The Community Learning Center does not label students by placing them in tracks that say to them, "You are not capable of learning what others can learn." Rather, the Center adheres to and practice the principle that all children can learn.

From my observation of programs designed for "gifted and talented" children, I have been struck by the obvious truth that all learners could benefit from such exciting programs. If only we could abandon the notion that all students must be tracked, we could begin to think about providing "gifted and talented" activities for all. My personal belief is that everyone is gifted and talented in some way, and that sorting people out by narrow definitions risks losing sight of what each is able to accomplish.

The work of Howard Gardner (1995) and others in describing the multiple intelligences of children can help us better understand the process of learning. Gardner proposes eight kinds of intelligence: musical; logical/mathematical; interpersonal; intrapersonal; bodily/kinesthetic; linguistic;

spatial; and naturalistic (the ability to recognize species of plants or animals in one's environment). In Gardner's view,

> [I]t is more important to discover areas of strength and to build on them than it is to fret too much about areas of weakness. It's important to watch each child carefully, to respect his or her strengths and weaknesses. If a parent or teacher decides to help the child work on something, it should be done in a sensitive and supportive way. If we follow this route, what we often find is that the child is actually more capable than we had thought! (*Early Childhood Today*, 1995, p. 32)

The Community Learning Center may have learners from all age groups, from elementary school through high school, with each student pursuing the student's own educational interests at the student's own level. I would hope that we could agree on new names to replace the old designations, which imply a hierarchy, with high school on top and more important that the rest. Perhaps communities can come up new names that make more sense than "elementary," "middle," and "high" school.

A few years ago, I visited a school in Australia that allowed adult students to sit alongside high school students and take courses they had missed in their youth. The result was a rich environment that enhanced learning for both the younger students and the adults. Similarly, parents who lack basic skills could come to the Community Learning Center to practice taking the GED test in order to obtain a high school equivalency certificate. Retired community members might be there to learn new skills or hobbies, and staff members from a community service agency might come to participate in a teleconference training session.

One way to grasp this concept is to think of the Community Learning Center as a center for community learning that also serves as a school. Some educators may feel more comfortable with the reverse description: a school that also serves as a center for community learning. The important point is that the new school would serve a wide range of community needs. Rather than detracting from the role of educating children, as some would have us believe, an expanded role would bring to the task the synergy generated by a learning community.

THE TEACHING AND LEARNING PROCESS

Constructivism is an approach to teaching and learning that is attracting growing interest and support. This approach is based on the idea that students can construct new understandings about the world they live in, and that each new understanding will build on previous ones and result from a growing complexity of thought.

Researcher Linda Darling-Hammond (1993, p. 754) describes the teacher's job in this approach as no longer being to "cover the curriculum," but rather to empower learners to develop their diverse talents. Darling-Hammond describes how teachers can use constructivism to reach curriculum goals:

> To foster meaningful learning, teachers must construct experiences that allow students to confront powerful ideas whole. They must create bridges between the very different experiences of individual learners and the common curriculum goals. They must use a variety of approaches to build on the conceptions, cultures, interests, motivations, and learning modes of their students. They must understand how their students think as well as what they know.

Brooks and Brooks (1993) identify five principles of a constructivist approach to teaching and learning:

- Posing problems of emerging relevance to learners;
- Structuring learning around primary concepts (Big Ideas);
- Seeking and valuing students' points of view;
- Adapting curriculum to address students' suppositions; and

- Assessing student learning in the context of teaching.

The Business Roundtable (1991), an organization of the country's top corporations, would seem to approve of a constructivist approach to instruction. In a guide developed to help businesses become involved in restructuring education, the Roundtable recommends instruction that "encourages teamwork and creativity by having students solve problems together where there is no one right answer; [and] makes active learning a priority...." (p. 20)

USING COMMUNITY RESOURCES

A much-quoted African proverb describes what must happen to make the community-based classroom a reality: "It takes a whole village to raise a child." This saying means that the village must not only share its resources with the village's children but must accept responsibility for their growth and development. Each student in the Community Learning Center would have a community mentor—in addition to the child's parents or primary caregivers—who takes an interest in the student's intellectual and social development. I am aware that implementation of such mentorships is a monumental task: mentors would have to be recruited, screened, and trained before being matched up with students. A summary of the potential benefits of a mentorship program will help us focus on the worth of such an effort.

COMMUNITY MENTORSHIP BENEFITS

- Mentors can serve as advocates for the student.
- Mentors can become advocates for the public schools as they become involved stakeholders.
- Mentors can provide tutorial assistance as needed.
- Mentors can offer a connection between the classroom and the real world of the community.

- Mentors who have no school-age children will learn more about what schools are doing for students.

- Mentors can help students and teachers better understand the requirements of the workplace.

- Mentors can offer students structured experiences through which they can see their schoolwork applied in real-world settings.

THE CURRICULUM

Textbooks obviously have a place in schools, but they cannot be the sole source of the curriculum. I remember vividly a conversation I had with a superintendent on this subject some years ago. I had remarked that the curriculum had to have connections to the community, and that parents, teacher, and community members should be involved in developing it. Disagreeing, the superintendent opened a review copy of a textbook that happened to be lying on his desk. Pointing to the table of contents, he said, "There is our curriculum. That is what our teachers will be expected to cover. We don't need 'involvement' to figure that out."

More than 80 years ago, Dewey (1915, p. 53) identified some of the difficulties with that approach:

> If textbooks are used as the sole material, the work is much harder for the teacher, for besides teaching everything herself she must constantly repress and cut off the impulses of the child toward action. Teaching becomes an external presentation lacking meaning and purpose as far as the child is concerned.

Dewey was right on target. We still have teachers who are driven to "cover" an 18-chapter textbook in an 18-week semester because that is what is the system expects of them. It is little wonder that we lose students who either drop out or give up on learning.

Olson and Clark (1977, p. 105) recommended over two decades ago that the curriculum of the school be "life-centered," preparing young people for four major adult roles:

- Sex and family role—getting along with parents, siblings, and peers, finding a fulfilling sexual life, and deciding whether to create one's own family.
- Productive worker role—ability and willingness to earn an adequate living and to consume goods and services wisely.
- Civic role—obedience to just laws and, beyond that, active democratic participation in local, state, national, and world politics.
- Self-realization role—discovering and developing answers to such persistent, lifelong questions as: "Who am I? What do I want to be like? Where am I going in life, and why?"

Ernest Boyer (1995) of the Carnegie Foundation for the Advancement of Teaching presents a similar curriculum for elementary schools in *The Basic School: A Community for Learning*. Boyer's Basic School is built on "Core Commonalties," various fields of knowledge organized thematically. The eight themes under which academic subject matter would be organized and taught are:

- The life cycle
- The use of symbols
- Response to the aesthetic
- Membership in groups
- A sense of time and space
- Producing and consuming
- Connections with nature
- Living with a purpose

Boyer's Basic School includes a strong commitment to character development. His model suggests the affirmation of seven virtues: honesty, respect, responsibility, compassion, self-discipline, perseverance, and giving. Today's schools have typically avoided issues related to character and morality, at least in part because schools have been reluctant to engage the community in a dialogue that would lead to agreement about which moral values the community holds in common. Once that agreement has been reached, the curriculum can embrace those common values.

In recent years, the public has been highly critical of the schools' failure to teach children and young people the moral values necessary to maintain a just and peaceful society. Accurately or not, politicians use terms like "moral meltdown" and the "breakdown of civilization" to describe a pessimistic view of contemporary society. Commenting on the failure of schools to teach moral values, Amitai Etzioni (1993, p. 12) says:

> Schools are so overwhelmed simply by maintaining order and passing on elementary knowledge and skills that they have neither the time nor the inclination to attend to their most important mission: transmitting a core of values to the next generation.

Etzioni (1993, pp. 258–59) believes that schools ought to teach "those values that Americans share":

- The dignity of all persons must be respected.
- Tolerance is a virtue; discrimination is abhorrent.
- Peaceful resolution of conflict is superior to violence.
- Truth telling is in general morally superior to lying.
- Democratic government is morally superior to totalitarianism and authoritarianism.
- One ought to give a day's work for a day's pay.
- Saving for one's own and one's country's future is better than squandering one's income and relying on others to attend to one's future needs.

Summarizing, Etzioni says: "Education must be reorganized to achieve a better integration between work and schooling."

One promising approach to integrating schooling and work in the curriculum has been developed by Paul DeLargy and his colleagues in REAL Enterprises, Inc., Athens, Georgia. REAL Enterprises has helped schools across the country create community businesses that are actually operated by teachers and students. These enterprises become living laboratories in which students can apply lessons learned in the classroom. The businesses have included day care centers, community newspapers, and an antique railroad that features dinner tours.

The curriculum of the Community Learning Center is based on a holistic perspective, encompassing all of the programs offered at the Center for learners of all ages. There are no artificial boundary dividing the "regular" school from the "community" school, or the "day" school from the "night" school. The holistic approach emphasizes interdisciplinary instruction. An auto mechanics laboratory is used, for example, to help students understand geometry by measuring the size of an engine cylinder; physics students learn the principles and uses of torque by using a torque wrench. Writing skills are developed by preparing advertising copy for a school fund-raising activity, or by writing a review of a school musical, dramatic, or athletic event.

One key to the development of an interdisciplinary curriculum is finding the time for faculty members to meet and design integrated activities. Our current scheduling arrangements allow little time for teachers to have conversations with other teachers in their own subject areas or grade levels, and almost no time for them to cross departmental and grade-level boundaries. In contrast, teachers in other countries work with groups of students only 15 to 20 hours a week, and spend 20 to 30 hours a week working individually with students and parents, planning and consulting with other teachers, and developing curriculum and assessments (Darling-Hammond, 1993). One way to find more time for meeting and planning is to operate the Community Learning Center on a year-round schedule instead of continuing the present pattern of a two- or three-month summer shutdown. A fuller discussion of year-round schools is presented in Chapter 9.

DAILY ANNOUNCEMENTS IN A VIRTUAL LEARNING CENTER

The Minnesota New Country School (MNCS) is one of several charter schools that were part of the Community Learning Centers project of the New American Schools Development Corporation. It received assistance from Wayne Jennings at Designs for Learning and the staff of the Center for School Change at the University of Minnesota. The World Wide Web home page for MNCS provides a window into the learning process that is taking place there. There you can read its statement on "Community as a Place to Learn": "Students can no longer be fed information in the hope of learning. We make every effort to steward a partnership with businesses, government, farms, service agencies, and organizations to involve students in real-life, meaningful learning opportunities." MNCS goes on to list a description for Community Service, School/Business Partnerships, Apprenticeships, and Student Businesses/ Entrepreneurships that provide vehicles for student learning.

An on-line "Virtual Learning Center" provides daily announcements, Internet Web references (for teachers and students), links to student projects and an outline of the schools total curriculum. A look at one day's announcements found a notice about Presentation Nights where students make presentations of work projects they have completed (students are required to make four presentations each year). There was also a notice about an opportunity for someone to complete a "short community service project" by installing a lock. And there was a notice directing students to make sure that portfolios for a year's curriculum are turned into their advisor when they are completed.

There are also Web pages where students presented their work. The work displayed ranged from a project on the Great Barrier Reef to an impressive project on a Civil War reenactment featuring the 14th Brooklyn New York State Militia. To learn more about the Minnesota New Country School in Le Sueur, Minnesota, visit its Web page at http://www.mncs. k12.mn.us.

Interdisciplinary teams of teachers, given the precious commodity of time, will invent marvelous experiences for their students—experiences that will result in learning that really is applicable to the real world.

If there is nothing else that we model to our students, I think we need to model that moment of ambiguity: that ability to leave questions raised but unanswered, that ability to listen to opposing views without choosing a side, that ability to speak passionately about ones position while acknowledging that perhaps, somewhere down the line, that position might change. When we can model this, we can provide a place where students can feel encouraged to speak and even to engage in conflict without simultaneously feeling that each conflict will have a winner and a loser.

Phyllis M. Ryder (1994, p. 2)

REFERENCES

Brooks, Jacqueline G., and Martin G. Brooks. 1993. *In Search of Understanding: The Case for Constructivist Classrooms.* Alexandria, VA: Association for Supervision and Curriculum Development.

Boyer, Ernest L. 1995. *The Basic School.* Princeton, NJ: Carnegie Foundation.

Bullard, Pamela, and Barbara O. Taylor. 1993. *Making School Reform Happen.* Needham Heights, MA: Allyn & Bacon.

Cohill, Andrew M., and others. 1995. *Managing the Evolution of a Virtual School in the Blacksburg Electronic Village.* Unpublished manuscript.

Darling-Hammond, Linda. 1993. "Reframing the School Reform Agenda," *Phi Delta Kappan,* June.

Designs for Learning. 1995. "A New Design for American Education," *The Brain Based Education/Learning Styles Networker,* 7, 2.

Dewey, John. 1900. *Dewey on Education*. New York: Teachers College, Columbia University.

Dewey, John. 1915. *The School and Society*. Chicago: University of Chicago Press.

Early Childhood Today. 1995. "Howard Gardner on Multiple Intelligences." August/September.

Etzioni, Amitai. 1993. *The Spirit of Community: Rights, Responsibilities, and the Communitarian Agenda*. New York: Crown.

Gardner, Howard. 1995. *Leading Minds*. New York: Basic Books.

Gardner, John W. 1981. *Self Renewal: The Individual and the Innovative Society*. New York: W. W. Norton.

Hart, Joseph K. 1913. *Educational Resources of Village and Rural Communities*. New York: Macmillan.

Impact II: The Teachers Network. 1991. *Teachers' Vision of the Future of Education: A Challenge to the Nation*. New York.

Olson, Edward G., and Phillip A. Clark. 1977. *Life-Centering Education*. Midland, MI: Pendell Publishing.

Ryder, Phyllis M. 1994. "Giving or Taking Authority: Exploring the Ideologies of Collaborative Learning." Paper presented at Conference on College Composition and Communication (annual meeting, Nashville, March 16).

6

COMMUNITY
TECHNOLOGY CENTERS

Technology is advancing at a pace faster than the world has ever known. If you have any doubt about the explosion of technology, log on to the Internet. On the World Wide Web (WWW) you'll find such things as NASA's description of its latest space mission, complete with video clips. Had you been logged on to the America's Cup home page in 1996, you would have seen pictures of a sinking racing sloop less than 24 hours after the mishap occurred. The 1998 Winter Olympics' home page gave the results of many events long before they were broadcast on tape-delay in the United States. Notices about college courses are broadcast over a satellite system regularly, providing access to potential students in more than a quarter of the world's northern hemisphere.

The shift from an industrial to an information society has not been achieved without pain. One serious concern is the inequality of access to the tools of technology—a sensitive issue that I raised at a conference of the International Community Education Association in Dublin, Ireland, almost a decade ago. In a group discussion of how community educators should address the problem of illiteracy, I suggested that the rapid spread of personal computers in the homes of the afflu-ent would widen the gap between educational "haves" and "have nots" in the United States. A professor from India rose, turned to me, and said: "Sir, I am offended by the question you raise. In my country many of the villages are so poor that the greatest technology they have is one battery-powered ra-dio for the whole village. Now you are talking about comput-ers!" I was sufficiently embarrassed to keep quiet for the rest of the session. But the reality is that in our society the wealth of a child's family is very likely to determine that child's ac-cess to educational tools.

Nowhere is this technology gap more evident than in the classrooms of our public schools and in the homes of the stu-dents who attend those schools. I have seen more sophisti-cated technology in some public elementary and secondary schools than I have on the campus of a typical college or uni-versity. And I have visited schools that appear to have been almost untouched by technology—whose teachers rely strict-ly on textbooks and chalkboards. Some students in those schools may have personal computers with CD-ROMs, mo-dems, and laser printers in their homes, while other students have none of these tools. It should not be surprising that most schools with high levels of technology in the classroom are lo-cated in affluent communities. Unfortunately, access to tech-nology lags far behind what it could or should be in almost every school.

The *Survey of Advanced Telecommunications in U.S. Public Schools* (U.S. Department of Education, 1995) reported dis-turbing data:

- ◆ Only 50 percent of U.S. public schools have access to the Internet (although this percentage is up from 35 percent a year earlier).

- ◆ Only 31 percent of schools with a large popula-tion of students from poor families (71 percent or more of students are eligible for free or reduced-price lunch) have access to the Internet, com-pared to 62 percent of schools with relatively few students from poor families (less than 11 percent eligibility).

- Lack of funding is the most frequently cited barrier to advanced telecommunications equipment in public schools. Other barriers in order of their reported importance are:
  - Lack of or poor equipment.
  - Too few access points in building.
  - Telecommunications equipment not easily accessible.
  - Telecommunication links not easily available.
  - Lack of adequately trained staff.
- In only 40 percent of the public schools that have computers with telecommunication capabilities, were the computers located in classrooms. The types of telecommunications most often located in classrooms were broadcast television and cable television.
- While 75 percent of public schools have access to some kind of computer network, only 49 percent have access to a wide area network (35 percent to the Internet, and 14 percent to such networks as CompuServe, America Online, and Prodigy).
- Smaller schools (less than 300 students) are less likely to be connected to the Internet than schools with larger enrollments.
- Internet capabilities (e-mail, newsgroups, resource location services, and graphical user interface) are more often available for teachers and administrators than for students.
- Only 6 percent of public schools have access to two-way video with two-way audio, and only 10 percent have access to one-way video with two-way audio (generally through satellite television reception).

AFTER SCHOOL TECHNOLOGY PROGRAMS FOR ALL COMMUNITY LEARNERS

At Hawthorne School in Seattle, Washington, the computer lab is open to all K-12 students and adults after school hours. Over 300 community residents have used this facility each year since the practice began in 1993. The labs are open from 3:00 p.m. to 8:00 p.m. Monday through Thursday.

Middle and high school students use the school's computers and tools (the Internet, CD-ROMS, and word processors) to access the electronic resources needed to complete their homework. On Tuesday evenings, an Internet course attracts both adults and students to the school.

The program is responsible for extending learning beyond the school day for many Hawthorne students. One unique outcome of the program has been elementary students working together with family members and peers. Having parents and older adults work with children has provided some powerful role models for learning.

The Seattle program is made possible through contributions from many businesses and community organizations and the Seattle Public Schools System, but volunteers from the school and community staff the computer lab. You can learn more about Hawthorne School's programs by visiting its Web page at http://www.hawthorneway.com/hawhorne.htm.

- ◆ Of schools with access to a wide area network, only 20 percent offer training to parents, 70 percent to administrators, 71 percent to teachers, and 52 percent to students.

In another survey, the American Electronics Association (1995) found a higher than expected level of technology deployment in schools, but lagging classroom access. The Association found that 48 percent of librarians but only 20 percent of teachers are connected to the Internet. The study found the same constraints that the U.S. Department of Education had identified: lack of money, lack of equipment, and inadequate training.

In the Community Learning Center, the latest information technology is available for teachers and students in the "regular"—that is, traditional—academic program. The same technology is available at appropriate times to parents, other family members, students, and members of the general community. It makes no sense to lock the doors on the technology in our schools when it could be made accessible to the extended community. Most of today's technology does not wear out with use; in most cases, it becomes obsolete long before it is worn out.

THE ELECTRONIC VILLAGE

The town I live in is being developed as a model "electronic village." Anyone who lives in Blacksburg, Virginia, may have access to a powerful computer network that will take them onto the information super highway. Most of us who have ventured out onto that highway have already sensed what a wonderful resource it can be for teachers and learners. So far, more than 70 percent of Blacksburg's households have signed up with the Blacksburg Electronic Village (known locally as BEV); BEV's homepage is found on the Internet at http://www.bev.net.

BEV is a collaborative venture of the town government, the Virginia Polytechnic and State University (Virginia Tech), and the regional telephone company. Randall Rothernberg (1996), in a feature article in Esquire magazine, wrote, "In the electronic village of Blacksburg, Virginia, the homes are wired, the students are on-line, and you can jack into the local pizza parlor."

Joe Wiencko, the original manager of BEV, describes its purpose:

> The goal of the project is to enhance the quality of people's lives by electronically linking the residents of the community to each other, to

worldwide networks, and to information resources in new and creative ways. The entire community of Blacksburg is being used as a real-life
laboratory to develop a prototype residential street
plan for the countrywide data superhighway being discussed as a high priority on the national
agenda. The project is being conducted so that its
most successful aspects can rapidly be replicated
in future electronic villages in the state of Virginia
and elsewhere in the United States. (Cohill et al.,
1995, p. 1)

When you sign up with the Electronic Village, you receive
software that allows you to:

- Send and receive e-mail messages worldwide.
- Browse the Internet for databases and graphic im-
  ages from throughout the world.
- Download files containing full-text documents
  from computers located in libraries, universities,
  and government agencies.
- Log on to a remote computer site on which you
  have an account.
- View such things as paintings from the Louvre in
  Paris.
- Join discussion groups about subjects that inter-
  est you.
- Register opinions on such local issues as the loca-
  tion of a new road or subdivision.
- Check current movie listings.
- Place a grocery order and have it delivered the
  same day.
- Pay bills and transfer funds.

A LiNC WITH THE COMMUNITY

Classrooms often contain many distractions to the learner, but not one classroom in Auburn Middle and High School (Montgomery County, VA). These students are too busy designing kites, building a mock roller coaster, or holding video teleconferences over computers to be distracted. "It's really interesting because we're talking to someone who is not in the room," said Amanda Mills, 14, a member of the aerodynamics team. She and two others in her group were talking to a Virginia Tech professor about kites—the group's project for the year. "We were talking about force, drag, weight, and different surfaces to use to increase velocity," said team member Danny Burroughs, 13. "It's a lot more helpful and easier than writing back and forth on e-mail." (Lu, *Roanoke Times*, May 17, 1998, p. NRV 22)

Once a week during the school year the eighth-grade physical science class uses live computer video links to talk with Tech professors, professionals from the community, and students at other schools. The computer-supported sound and video transmissions are of good quality if you don't mind a occasional delays and breaks. Most of the students don't seem to notice.

The project that supports this approach is Learning in Networked Communities (LiNC). It involves four schools in Montgomery County Virginia (Auburn High, Auburn Middle, Blacksburg High, and Blacksburg Middle). The goal of the LiNC project, which is sponsored by a grant from the National Science Foundation, is to promote interaction between children at different schools and between the community and its schools. "We want to pull the county together and equalize opportunities between all kids," said John Carroll, director of LiNC. He is also head of the Tech computer science department. "By using technology, we can bring the community into the classroom and make people available to kids in the schools, people who do not have the time to go there." (Lu, 1998, p. NRV23)

THE VIRTUAL SCHOOL

As part of a National Science Foundation project, the College of Human Resources and Education and the Computer Science Department at Virginia Tech are working with the county schools to develop a network-based virtual school, which is defined as:

> [A]n unbounded educational environment with no walls, no halls, no bells, where (virtual) collaborative classrooms encompass the entire community and exploit connections among diverse educational resources—schools, libraries, homes, businesses, government, local and global networks, and individuals. We are working toward an educational system that extends beyond the physical school into the community, in which both parents and their children continue to communicate, to learn, and to collaborate in a rich network environment. (Cohill et al., 1995, p. 3)

From the days of John Dewey, enlightened educators have tried to find ways to break down the walls that shut student learning off from the real world beyond the school—the world in which knowledge taught in school has its origins and applications. The virtual school is one means of taking learning far beyond the confines of a school, or even a community.

In the electronic village, the local school system has its own homepage, as does each individual school. The schools have an even greater presence on the Internet, because many classes have their own homepage where student work is exhibited for viewing by parents and other interested community members.

Another project, "PCs for Families," a collaborative effort of Virginia Tech's Computer Science Department and Riner Elementary School in Montgomery County, Virginia, is studying the effect of access to networked computing by both students and parents on the long-term academic achievement of students. Families of the students randomly selected to participate in the project were given computers and mo-dems to access the Internet. Participating parents agreed to attend training sessions and to support their children's educational use of the networked computers.

PROVIDING ACCESS

One factor driving the development of telecommunications technology is the emerging competition between telephone and cable television companies to provide a full range of data, voice, and video services. The federal government, in its regulatory role, will be a key player as the nation's delivery system for telecommunications continues to evolve. The Telecommunications Act of 1996 aims to remove barriers to competition in all areas of telecommunications by limiting government regulation and encouraging competition, while at the same time trying to guarantee affordable rates to consumers in all parts of the country.

The Federal Communications Commission (FCC) has ruled that schools and libraries are entitled to discounts that range from 20 to 90 percent on telecommunications services; these special "E-rates" will reduce the cost of networked computing for all schools, with the largest discounts going to the poorest schools.

COMMUNITY LEARNING AND INFORMATION NETWORK

Another approach to the development of technology for teaching and learning is the Community Learning and Information Network (CLIN) project headed by former U.S. Assistant Commissioner of Education William Pierce. The vision of CLIN, a nonprofit corporation, is to create a community-linked learning and information delivery system that will give all Americans equal access to the education, training, and information required for lifelong learning and skill development. The project's ambitious goals include improving workforce skills; restructuring education and training; increasing global competitiveness; promoting business development; and improving the delivery of heathcare and other social services (Community Learning and Information Network, 1994).

CLIN's aim is to link every public and private school, every institution of higher education, and a great number of corporate and industrial training sites. Each CLIN site will initially consist of two classrooms:

- ◆ A computer-aided instruction classroom, which will give students and teachers access to extensive libraries of computerized instructional materials that can be geared to the learning pace of individual students.

- ◆ A two-way interactive televideo classroom, which will bring expert instructors from across town and across the world into face-to-face interaction with students in traditional classroom settings.

The CLIN model is based on a public-private partnership. It proposes a new "shared usage" concept under which communities can pay for the system and equipment by selling excess time to industry and government users on a fee-for-service basis, thereby reducing the training and education costs associated with the use of such sophisticated technology as teleconferencing. An accounting package supplied by CLIN monitors and reports usage and prepares invoices. Revenues from this shared use will allow the local CLIN site to become self-sufficient.

Another feature of the CLIN model is, with government and industry agreeing to use the local CLIN site, states and communities can guarantee self-liquidating bonds to be sold in the private market that will provide the necessary capital to purchase the technology to equip community learning centers. The CLIN designers have developed a shared-usage business model for the first prototype sites that project revenue generation within six months. The Community Learning Center will offer citizens the opportunity to learn how to use information age technologies.

VIRTUAL REALITY

The Community Learning Center will make extensive use of the new technology known as virtual reality, which involves wearing special goggles and gloves. The goggles are actually two television screens that project images to each of your eyes. The goggles are equipped with motion sensors that respond to head movement by adjusting the images. Special "datagloves" have built-in sensors that respond to hand movement. A fast, image-calculating computer completes the needed equipment.

To use the virtual reality equipment, you call up an image that is really a set of two images projected on the goggle lenses in a way that gives a three-dimensional effect. As you move your head, the computer resets the images based on its calculation of how your movement would affect what you are seeing. With your dataglove, you can "touch" and move things around within the images you are viewing. The dataglove senses your hand movements, and the computer projects an image of your hand in the field of vision of your goggles, allowing you to manipulate the objects you are looking at. The computer can alter these images at the rate of 15 to 30 times a second.

With virtual reality it will be possible for students to travel through the human body, watching the heart pump blood, or dissect a frog without smelling formaldehyde. It will be possible to look at the nucleus of a molecule or the electrons of an element, or take a trip to Appomattox, Virginia, to participate in Lee's surrender and the end of the Civil War. Futurist Joel Barker (1992, p. 197) wrote, "Via virtual reality the entire communication/information industry will be fundamentally altered." That is not hard to believe.

PUBLISHING PROJECTS

My sister is a media specialist at an elementary school just outside Houston, Texas, who has managed to develop a fairly well-equipped technology center on a very limited school budget. Although her background is in library science, she has become the technology expert at her school. Beginning with one computer, then adding another, the media center gradually acquired a laser printer, a CD-ROM, and other equipment. The challenge was how to make the best use of too few computers to meet the needs of the entire student body.

Working with a group of interested parents, the school designed a publishing project that involves students, teachers, and parents. Students are encouraged to undertake all kinds of creative writing and the parent volunteers enter the student writing on a computer, formatting it for desktop publishing. Together, teachers, students, and parents produce finished books that are distributed throughout the school and community. Seeing their work in print has been a tremendous source of pride for the students.

PARENT EDUCATION

A community center for technology suggests extraordinary opportunities to engage parents in educational activities. The Community Learning Center will regularly hold evening and weekend sessions for parents, who can learn what their children are learning in school, or receive help with their own basic educational needs and interests. In a supportive environment, even parents who are initially intimidated by computers can overcome their anxieties and become hooked on learning. Later, child development and job skill classes can be added to the class offerings.

COMPUTING SENIORS

"Computing Seniors" is a program that is helping Roanoke, Virginia, schools connect with another important segment of the community. John Lensch, the principal of Highland Park Learning Center, saw the potential for using technology to help the school offer a valuable service to seniors in the community. The program at Highland Park was so successful it is replicated in 28 schools citywide.

A report in *Parade Magazine* (Ryan 1997) noted that Lensch expected only a modest response to his invitation to seniors to sign up for a computer class, and was astonished when his neighborhood flier attracted a class of 20 and a waiting list of 50. Lensch saw the program as "a way of paying back the community for the millions of dollars the people of Roanoke have invested in technology" (p. 22).

One forward-looking senior who signed up was the 70-year-old woman who runs the school cafeteria. She explained that she wanted to prepare herself for the introduction of computers in the cafeteria management business (Ryan, p. 23).

COMPUTER MASTERS VOLUNTEER PROGRAM

Several years ago, the Cooperative Extension Service in Virginia instituted Master Gardeners, which became a very successful program. Veteran gardeners who wanted to increase their gardening knowledge and skills could sign up for 50 hours of intensive instruction by horticulture experts from the state's land grant universities. In return for this training, the master gardeners agreed to provide 50 hours of training to interested gardening beginners in the community. Once they got involved, many veterans volunteered for many more than 50 hours.

The same approach might be used to develop a cadre of trained computer masters who would, after receiving training, become volunteer teachers of others. Some could work with students during the traditional school day, while others work with parents and other community members during evening hours and on weekends.

Many communities have residents who already have a high level of computer skills developed on the job. Other communities may have to identify business partners in order to find a pool of knowledgeable computer users who are willing to become involved in a computer masters program. There are often significant numbers of secondary school students who have the skills to qualify for such a program; many high school students are very effective in working with younger children or adults of various ages.

This approach to developing trained volunteers is a low-cost way to support the staffing of a technology center in the Community Learning Center. The Virginia Master Gardeners Program has such a strong reputation for high quality that there is almost always a waiting list for would-be masters/volunteers. A similar program for computer masters could produce similar results—in which case, of course, everyone wins.

HELLO? HELLO?

HOW ABOUT STARTING WITH A TELEPHONE?

An interesting thing happens in my classes almost every time we talk about the use of technology in the classroom. Teachers frequently point out that, while this high tech stuff sounds good, they would be extremely grateful to start with a telephone. When you think about it, it is hard to come up with an example of any other professional group in our society that doesn't have access to a personal telephone. In most businesses, a phone on the desk is as common as a stapler. If we really want teachers to be more active in connecting with parents and the rest of the community outside the classroom, we ought to be willing to supply them with that basic low-tech communication tool—the telephone!

REFERENCES

Barker, Joel A. 1992. *Paradigms: The Business of Discovering the Future*. New York: Harper Collins Publishers.

Cohill, Andrew M., Roger W. Ehrich, Deborah Hix, Andrea L. Kavanaugh, and Herman G. Bartlett. 1995. *Managing the Evolution of a Virtual School in the Blacksburg Electronic Village*. Unpublished manuscript.

Community Learning & Information Network. 1994. *The CLIN National Initiative: An Overview*. Washington, DC.

Daily Report Card. March 22, 1995. "Linking Both Sides of the Desk," Fairfax, VA: George Mason University.

Rothenberg, Randall. February 1996. "Life in Cyburbia," *Esquire*.

U.S. Department of Education, Office of Educational Research and Improvement. 1995. *The Survey of Advanced Telecommunications in U.S. Public Schools, K-12*. Washington, DC.

7

THE COLLABORATING COMMUNITY

True collaboration is a bit like the weather: it is a lot easier to talk about it than to do something about it. Schools have talked about becoming more collaborative for more than a decade, but few schools have gone beyond talking about it to actually become more collaborative. In many communities, a lot of time is spent going through the litany of why collaboration has not happened. Some of the frequently cited barriers to collaboration are:

- Fear of losing power and control.
- Rules, regulations, and policies.
- Institutional bureaucracies.
- Lack of collaborative skills.
- Systems that reward independent rather than collaborative efforts.
- Lack of the time needed to make collaboration work.

Many communities work hard at establishing a culture of collaboration between and among agencies, organizations, and institutions, while others make little effort to foster connections between groups. The status of collaboration in a community may be thought of as running along a continuum.

|_____|_____|_____|
No Relationship   Cooperation   Coordination   Collaboration

On one end of the continuum there is *no relationship* between any of the components of the community's set of resources. In communities at that end of the continuum, it is rare to find the leaders of agencies, organizations, or institutions engaged in any kind of conversation about the work of their groups and the needs of the community. There may even be competition for resources between organizations, so that, at times, organizations may be working at cross purposes in their efforts to receive more favorable treatment from those who control resources.

The next position on the continuum is *cooperation*, in which information flows between organizations but there is no other form of interaction. This kind of relationship may be thought of as "show and tell." There are frequent opportunities for the leadership of organizations to get together and share information about what they are doing, but no attempt to undertake joint effort. Observation has led me to believe that community organizations that have joint meetings revolving around eating together seldom make any serious attempt to work together. If eating lunch takes up half the time the organizations spend together, little time is left to go beyond the show-and-tell stage. Real collaboration takes much more time than cooperation.

Coordination, the next position on the continuum, provides a way for organizations to work together while retaining individual authority. A common mission links organizations in an informal relationship, and joint planning and a division of labor are needed to accomplish the shared mission. But coordination is too often limited to an agreement to stay out of each other's way when providing community programs and services.

In a community that has achieved *collaboration*, new structures were developed to manage the shared resources of multiple organizations. There is a commitment to share goals, responsibility, authority, accountability, resources, and rewards. Cynthia Marshall of Cities in Schools says, "The hardest part of collaboration is having people from diverse backgrounds learn to trust each other" (Melaville and Blank, 1993, p. 32). Trust is the underlying principle in all successful collaboration. Participants have to be able to say, "I am willing to trust others to do their part in making sure that we do not fail." In this chapter, we examine ways to build collaborative relationships in order to make the best use of a community's resources to solve its problems.

A FOUNDATION FOR SUCCESSFUL COLLABORATION

In the 1980s, I was asked to provide training and technical assistance to many communities that were involved in developing new collaborative organizations to serve their citizens. I found it helpful to use this set of simple components as the foundation for a collaborative effort:

- ◆ **Credibility**. The initiators of the collaborative effort must have a high level of credibility within the community.

- ◆ **Shared concerns**. Concerns that are shared across organizational boundaries are the force that brings organizations together.

- ◆ **Trust building**. Before any collaborative action can be taken, the partners must begin the process of building mutual trust.

- ◆ **Provision for bailout**. Each organization brought to the table to consider a collaborative effort should be able to exit gracefully if the emerging collaborative does not fit within that organization's mission.

- ◆ **Resources**. To be successful, every collaborative effort must have resources committed to its program of work.
- ◆ **Shared decision-making**. Decision making must be done openly through the participation of all partners.
- ◆ **Consensus process**. Consensus must be used to obtain the support of all partners.
- ◆ **Realistic early goals**. The early goals of a collaborative should be realistic and obtainable in a fairly short period of time in order to build momentum.
- ◆ **Evaluation**. A commitment must be made to evaluate the results of the collaborative effort.
- ◆ **Celebration**. Every success achieved by the collaborative should be celebrated.
- ◆ **Moving to a higher level**. As success is achieved in the initial stages, subsequent goals should be set at higher, more challenging levels.
- ◆ **Being ready to fold the tent**. As the reasons for the formation of the specific collaborative disappear, there may be a need for the collaborative to disband and move to other concerns, perhaps with other partners.

FULL SERVICE SCHOOLS VS. NEIGHBORHOOD-BASED COLLABORATION

There is currently some debate about the role that schools should play in the collaborative delivery of community services. Joy Dryfoos (1995) places schools at the center of a collaborative approach to service delivery. While Dryfoos does not often use the terms "community learning centers" or "community schools," she has become a leading advocate for a central role for schools in the delivery of community services for families and children.

Other voices in the debate favor neighborhood-based community services delivered through interagency collaboration, rather than school-based services. In the neighborhood-based approach, the school is just one equal member of a team of organizations. Capper (1994) found that the neighborhood-based approach represents a move beyond an "educentric" perspective that makes schools the focus of control and pedagogy apart from communities and families. The neighborhood-based model channels information about the needs of families and children into the school through the school's representative on the interagency team. Capper reports: "[T]he teams seek to take a global, holistic perspective of the community and family in relation to the student, rather than a narrow perspective that isolates student problems in the school." (p. 260)

A majority of the participants in the interagency model Capper studied believe that the collaborative should be neighborhood-based because such collaboration provides:

- Treatment at the core of student struggles (that is, within families and communities).

- Shared blame and responsibility for student problems.

- Increased accessibility of services.

- Personalized services for residents and a vehicle for agency public relations and outreach. (p. 262)

The theme that emerged from the Capper study was that a neighborhood-based effort results in sharing both blame and responsibility for students and their families.

A reasonable position to take in the debate over school-based vs. neighborhood-based service is that each community is different, both in the mix of resources it has available and in the needs of its residents. This difference implies that there may be more than one "best" way of bringing about collaboration in the delivery of community services. The most important point to recognize may be that some form of collaboration is needed to address the complex problems faced by students and their families today.

WHAT MAKES COLLABORATION WORK?

The Amherst H. Wilder Foundation sponsored a review of the research on factors that influence successful collaboration. Mattessich and Monsey (1992) identified sets of factors that were supported by studies done by other researchers. The following is a summary of the top factors identified in those studies; the number of studies mentioning each factor is given in parentheses.

- ◆ Factors Related to the Environment
  - History of collaboration or cooperation in the community. (6)
- ◆ Factors Related to Membership Characteristics
  - Mutual respect, understanding and trust. (11)
  - Appropriate cross section of members. (11)
  - Members see collaboration as in their self-interest. (6)
- ◆ Factors Related to Process/Structure
  - Members share a stake in both process and outcome. (6)
  - Multiple layers of decision making. (6)
  - Flexibility. (4)
  - Development of clear roles and policy guidelines. (4)
- ◆ Factors Related to Communication
  - Open and frequent communication. (9)
  - Established informal and formal communication links. (5)
- ◆ Factors Related to Purpose
  - Concrete, attainable goals and objectives. (5)
  - Shared vision. (4)
- ◆ Factors Related to Resources
  - Sufficient funds. (8)
  - Skilled convener. (7)

Although it would be hard to identify any one or two of these factors as more important than any of the others, I will comment on the influence that some of these factors have had on the success of a collaborative effort.

First, the factor of mutual respect, understanding, and trust has to be viewed as the foundation for everything that is undertaken. I continue to be amazed by how little most of us know about the various organizations that serve our communities. It is impossible to think about working together until we learn how each organization operates, the culture and values each possesses, and what can be expected from each one. The first agenda item in any attempt to build collaboration must be a process for sharing what each organization is all about, and for learning about the people who will represent it. It is often said, accurately, that organizations don't cooperate, people do. It has also been observed that collaboration is like dancing with an octopus.

SETTING THE GROUND RULES

Collaboratives need to decide:

- ♦ Where, when and how often will partners meet?
- ♦ How will partners share responsibility for organizing and leading the meetings?
- ♦ Who prepares and contributes to the agenda?
- ♦ What rules should guide the dialogue?
- ♦ Will partners make decisions by majority rule or consensus?
- ♦ What can partners do to ensure that decision making occurs inside the group and not behind the scenes?
- ♦ What happens if there is a problem or conflict?
- ♦ How will partners handle logistical arrangements?
- ♦ Under what circumstances should there be a third-party facilitator?

(Melaville and Blank 1993, p. 32)

HOW ONE COMMUNITY LEARNING CENTER FUNDS ITS PROGRAM

ANKENY COMMUNITY SCHOOLS, IA

The Community Education Department serves 5,000 students (K-12) and a community of 25,000. Programs are offered for all ages in nine Ankeny public schools and one community resource center. The estimated budget profile for the community learning center at Westwood Elementary School is as follows:

1. Part-time Community Education Coordinator:
   Salary $20,000
   Fringe $5,500

2. School-Age Child Care Program $68,000
   (100% funded by user fees)

3. After-School Enrichment Program $17,000
   (100% funded by PTA and registration fees)

4. Adult Education Classes $7,500
   (100% funded by registration fees)

5. Ankeny Substance Abuse Project $8,000
   Prevention presentations, staff/student/family direct client services; 25% funded by Safe and Drug-Free Schools and Communities Act, 75% funded by local voluntary contributions (no fees are charged to participants)

6. Ankeny Family Advocacy Project $8,000
Attendance and truancy program; juvenile court
liaison, in-home family counseling services, prevention program to reduce tobacco use, absenteeism, poor parenting, crime, violence, interaction
with gangs (no fees are charged to participants)

7. City Leisure Service $14,000
   Youth and adult recreation programs during
   evenings and weekends; 15% funded by city,
   10% by schools, 75% by fees

8. Community use of Westwood facilities $22,000
   YMCA, Scout groups and youth-serving organizations, Adult-Church-Community-
   Business requests for local, nonprofit purposes, private use reservations, 50% funded
   by schools, 50% funded by rental fees

9. Other programs unique to Westwood each
   year $3,000

Total program and administrative budget each
   year $173,000

Source: U.S. Department of Education
http://www.ed.gov/pubs/LearnCenters/finance.html

It is vitally important to get the right people to the table when collaboration is being developed. Organizers have to continually ask themselves, Do we have representatives from every segment of the community that will be affected by the work of this collaborative?

It should be obvious that open and frequent communication is required to make any collaborative effort work, but it may be less obvious that this kind of communication takes careful planning and a lot of work. Far too often, collaborative efforts fail before they even get started because the organizers did not place a high enough value on communicating with potential collaborators. Like a living organism, collaboration needs air and sunshine to grow. A collaborative organization is organic in nature and must be nurtured and attended to if it is to flourish.

Another critical factor in the success or failure of collaborative effort is having a skilled convener. I will never forget my experience while serving on a planning committee made up of representatives of two statewide organizations that had decided to hold a first-ever joint conference. The planning committee worked very hard to identify common interests and goals and had taken pains to assure that the two organizations would feel equal ownership of the joint meeting. But the committee's hard work went up in smoke at the opening session, when the president of one of the organizations— someone who had not been involved in the planning—rose to open the conference. Her first words welcomed the members of the other organization to her group's conference. With a few words she destroyed the feeling of collaborative effort and shared purpose the committee had tried hard to create.

Conveners of any kind of collaborative effort have to be constantly aware of the tightrope they walk. They must make every effort to allow all participants to bring their resources to the table, join in the collaborative effort, and still maintain their viability as individual organizations. Years ago, when I was promoting the idea of having Cooperative Extension agents deliver their programs through school-based community education programs, the Dean of Extension at my university warned me that I was going to be in big trouble if, after our agents delivered programs, people walked out of the classrooms saying, "Aren't community schools wonderful for providing us with all this useful instruction at no charge?" He pointed out that he had to go to the state capital every year to justify the budget request for state Extension funding. If the public perception was that the community schools were providing these services, it was going to be hard for him to keep funds in place to support the organization and the programs. This issue becomes especially real in times of scarce resources. The solution is to make sure that every organization that contributes gets recognized.

COLLABORATIVE EXAMPLES

SCHOOL-BASED HEALTH CENTERS

One of the earliest collaborations in the pioneering Flint, Michigan, community schools was the Healthy Child Program, in which the local children's hospital teamed with the schools to give periodic health checks to all students and to provide some medical and dental care to children whose families could not afford to take care of their health care needs.

Today, we are seeing a renewal of the idea of using schools as centers for the delivery of health care for children and families. The National Health and Education Consortium (1995, p. 1) proposed the establishment of health centers in elementary schools:

> One of public education's major challenges is coping with the health status—mental and physical —of its students and the impact of their health on their ability to learn. For decades educators and policy makers have discussed school and curriculum reform as vehicles for improving educational outcomes for our students. Increasingly, schools are acknowledging that education reform cannot occur without focusing on the other interrelated needs of families and children. Schools must commit themselves to both educating and helping build a foundation for learning.

Multidisciplinary teams of professionals working in school health centers provide students with onsite primary and preventative health care, mental health counseling, health promotion, referral, and follow-up services. The teams include nurse practitioners, physicians, social workers, nurses, and health educators.

Funding for school-based health centers usually comes from a combination of private and public grants. Private sources include foundations, service organizations in the community, and third-party reimbursements. Public funds generally come from state and local human and social service funds, Maternal and Child Health block grants, Medicaid, and other sources. A 1993 survey by the Center for Population Options (1994) found that the average annual budget for school-based health centers was close to $170,000.

Clinics can help prevent such school-related problems as absenteeism, poor learning outcomes, truancy, and dropping out. But schools cannot assume sole responsibility for the delivery of health and social services in addition to all of their other responsibilities. The National Health and Education Consortium (1995, p. 6) made this point explicitly:

> Already often overburdened, teachers need help educating children, not additional pressures and regulations. That is exactly what elementary school-based health centers are designed to do: help teachers to teach by seeing that their sick, hungry, or frightened students get the attention they need from qualified health experts to ensure that they return to the classroom faster and better able to learn.

Partnerships between schools and the health care community contribute significantly to success in the schools' primary mission of educating the children.

WALBRIDGE CARING COMMUNITIES (ST. LOUIS)

Housed in inner-city St. Louis, Walbridge Caring Communities is working to create a sense of community to counteract the effects that drugs, poverty, alienation, unemployment, and a host of other ills have had on families. With an interdisciplinary staff of 22, the program provides a broad range of services, but the program is not just about delivering services, it also tries to strengthen values.

The fundamental idea underlying this initiative is that "children live in families; families live in communities; therefore, to help children, one must help families and communities" (Melaville and Blank, 1993, p. 95). Assisted by the Danforth Foundation, the project grew out of conversations between the commissioner of education and the directors of the departments of Social Services, Mental Health, and Health. Keith Schafer, director of the department of Mental Health, describes their beginnings:

> In the urban settings...we all felt helpless and somewhat inadequate. We said, "Why don't we pick a school setting and offer our services, set up a community advisory board, hire a person they trust, and serve as partners, as opposed to telling them what they should be doing." (Melaville and Blank, 1993, p. 96)

The program is based on the idea that families are best served by a "seamless system" of community services. The goals of the collaborative effort are linked to the education of the children of the community. Briefly stated, those goals are:

- ◆ To keep children in school while increasing their level of success in school
- ◆ To keep children safe in their homes
- ◆ To avoid the breakup of families
- ◆ To keep children out of the juvenile justice system

The program is directed by a local board made up of one-fourth each of parents, school staff, representatives of partner institutions, and community leaders. Walbridge Elementary School, with about 530 students in grades K through 5, is the central focus of the program. Community needs were identified through a series of meetings and door-to-door canvassing. The needs identified included concern about crime and drugs; the need of parents to occasionally get away from children; the lack of wholesome activities for teenagers; the need for parent education; and the need for all-day care for young children. Those needs led to programs and services designed to meet them:

- Families First, an intensive intervention for families in crisis.
- Case management, which links families to social services and provides direct help such as parenting education and tutoring for the children.
- Day treatment, providing behavior therapy for children with problems.
- Substance abuse counseling, a program in which counselors work with families before, during, and after treatment.
- Student assistance, which includes after-school tutoring and classroom presentations on topics such as self-esteem and self-perception.
- Latchkey, a combination of recreational and academic activities before and after school.
- Youth center, offering Friday evening recreational and educational programs for children aged 5 to 19.
- Parents as Teachers, an early screening and parent education program for families of newborns to three-years-old.
- Health services, from first aid to transportation to treatment facilities.

One indicator that Walbridge Caring Communities is having an impact is an increase in parent involvement at the elementary school. The principal estimates that involvement has doubled since the program started. An antidrug task force, formed in the wake of two drive-by shootings, conducts antidrug marches twice a month.

The Caring Communities initiative cannot solve all the problems of its inner-city urban community, but it has definitely made a start. Bringing service agencies together to work with the community in providing needed services is a big accomplishment in a world in which each independent bureaucracy tries to provide what it thinks people need, with little connection either to other providers or to the people themselves.

For more information, contact the Walbridge Caring Communities Program, 5019 Alcott, St. Louis, MO 03120.

WASHINGTON HEIGHTS COMMUNITY SCHOOLS (NEW YORK CITY)

The Children's Aid Society (CAS), working with the New York City Board of Education, used the community education process to develop an urban model community school that has many of the characteristics of the Community Learning Center proposed in this book. In answer to the question, "What is special about your program?," the Children's Aid Society (1995, p. 1) offers this answer:

> The community school concept turns public schools into full-service community centers that are open all day, all week, year-round, with onsite health and dental clinics, mental health counseling, child care, extended-day programs, tutoring, adult education, parent workshops, cultural programs, and summer camp. The daytime academic curriculum is fully integrated with the before-, after-school, and evening programs, and the schools are open to everyone in the community—children, siblings, teens, parents, and other adults.

The comprehensiveness of this program is impressive. Services and extracurricular activities are not provided as "add-ons" to the traditional educational programs of the school but are integrated into its daily functioning. The Washington Heights educators and service providers are working together to achieve the same goals for students. CAS explains that the purpose of the community school is to provide children the full range of services they need to enter classrooms ready to learn, and to give parents the help they need to support their children's education and healthy growth and development.

In many integrated service models, the service providers come into the school as guests. They remain separate from the academic functions of the "regular" program, and their presence often has little effect on those functions. Too often, the day school belongs to the educators, and the after-school and weekend programs and services belong to social service or community-based agencies. In the Washington Heights model, "co-ownership" defines the relationship between the school district and CAS. In those schools, "both educators and CAS staff shape both the academic and nonacademic aspects of the children's time in school, so that children experience a seamless school day as they move between these different components of their school" (Children's Aid Society, 1995, p. 10).

For more information about the Washington Heights Community Schools program, contact the Children's Aid Society, 105 East 22nd Street, New York, NY 10010.

NEW BEGINNINGS (SAN DIEGO)

New Beginnings began as an attempt by four agencies to collaborate to improve the lot of families. The agencies were San Diego City, San Diego County, San Diego City Schools, and San Diego Community College District. They were later joined by San Diego Housing Commission, the University of California–San Diego School of Medicine, San Diego Children's Hospital, and IBM Corporation.

The agencies' agreement to focus on the family was based on the assumption that the problems of children are part of a mosaic. They believed that few problems can be solved without addressing other problems, and that no agency would be successful acting in isolation.

A center was established at an elementary school to provide a home for a score of community agencies. Melaville and Blank (1993, p. 108) describe how the agencies work together:

> The representatives are expected to leave behind their parochial origins and become family service advocates, brokering public services to meet the full range of a family's needs. They also provide some direct services like immunizations, school registration, and counseling. Instead of working

side by side, they are expected to work together. Instead of limiting the scope of their work with families, they are encouraged to become more deeply involved, and instead of the usual porous arms-length bureaucracies, the center provides something more like a bear hug.

New Beginnings is about fundamental reform in the way services to children and families are provided. It attacks both the human and bureaucratic boundaries that, in the past, were obstacles to providing a level of service that would give families a chance to become self-sufficient. The foundation for the entire effort is simple: "Families, as the primary caregivers, must be supported and strengthened" (Melaville and Blank, 1993, p. 109). The goals of the collaborative effort are to improve the health, social and emotional well-being, and academic achievement of the children; to promote greater self-sufficiency and involvement of families; and to use a unified approach and philosophy among institutions that will lead to greater cost-efficiency and effectiveness.

OTHER COMMUNITIES

Other collaborative communities are emerging. They have in common several elements that must be incorporated in the design of the Community Learning Center:

- Collaborating agencies and organizations must work as equal partners, sharing all aspects of their joint effort.

- Services must focus on families in order to have an effect on children and their ability to benefit from educational programs.

- Educational, social, and community services must be integrated into a seamless experience for children and their families.

- The issue of "school-based" as opposed to "school-linked" services is not as important as the question of how each individual community can make the best use of its resources to improve the quality of education and life.

♦ Collaborative partnerships are based on trust and understanding that must be consciously developed over time.

It is crucial not to lose sight of the fact that collaboration takes place among people, not institutions. People must be the focus of every collaborative effort; they must be given adequate planning time and support services, and must be rewarded for positive collaborative behavior. Without support from their institutions, the people who are vital to the process will be unwilling to invest themselves in making collaboration happen.

Lisbeth Schorr (1997, p. 382) provides valuable insight into the need for collaborating communities:

> Society must be able to count on parents to have the moral sense, the beliefs, and the capacity to assume [their]...responsibilities. But, as we give heavy weight to relying on parents to carry out their obligations, we must all be aware that individual parents cannot meet their responsibilities in our complex, twenty-first century world without support from outside. Collectively, we must make sure that the societal structures that can support families, and that can strengthen communities are in place.

REFERENCES

Capper, Colleen A. 1994. "We're Not Housed in an Institution, We're Housed in the Community," *Educational Administration Quarterly*, 30, 3, 257–77.

Center for Population Options. 1994. *School-Based and School-Linked Health Centers, Update 1993*. Washington, DC: Advocates for Youth.

Children's Aid Society. 1995. *Proposal for a Longitudinal Evaluation of the Washington Heights Community Schools Project*. Unpublished manuscript. New York.

Dryfoos, Joy G. 1994. *Full-Service Schools*. San Francisco: Jossey-Bass.

Mattessich, Paul G., and Barbara R. Monsey. 1993. *Collaboration: What Makes it Work.* St. Paul, MN: Amherst H. Wilder Foundation.

Melaville, T., and M. Blank. 1993. *Together We Can: A Guide for Crafting a Pro-Family System of Education and Human Services.* Washington, DC: Government Printing Office.

National Health and Education Consortium. 1995. *Putting Children First: State-Level Collaboration Between Education and Health.* Washington, DC.

Schorr, Lisbeth. 1997. *Common Purpose: Strengthening Families and Neighborhoods to Rebuild America.* New York: Doubleday.

8

DEVELOPING COMMUNITY

We cannot underestimate the effect that the community has on the education that takes place in the Community Learning Center. No one has described that relationship more eloquently than Joseph K. Hart (1913, p. 9):

> No child can escape his community. He may not like his parents, or the neighbors, or the ways of the world. He may groan under the processes of living, and wish he were dead. But he goes on living, and he goes on living in the community. The life of the community flows about him, foul or pure; he swims in it, drinks it, goes to sleep in it, and wakes to the new day to find it still about him. He belongs to it; it nourishes him, or starves him, or poisons him; it gives him the substance of his life. And in the long run it takes its toll of him, and all he is.

The Community Learning Center is committed to using its resources to improve the quality of life in the communities where they exist.

Communities are inseparably tied to the institutions that serve them. The school is a part of the community, and the community is a part of the school. The Community Learning Center takes an active role in developing the community as an investment in the education of the children and youth.

We live in an age marked by divisiveness and confrontation. Groups organized around one cause or another pit themselves against one another in alarming numbers. In politics, conservatives and liberals point fingers and call each other names. Religious groups wage wars, each group believing it alone is right. Conflict exists between labor and management, rich and poor, blacks and whites, armed militias and the government, Christians and Jews, citizens and immigrants—and the list could go on. What we are witnessing, not just locally but nationally and internationally, is a culture of divisiveness.

A community divided by issues such as race, politics, wealth, and culture is a community weakened and struggling. Energy that could be spent making positive change is consumed in the effort to maintain conflict. Bill Cirone (1995), long-time superintendent of schools in Santa Barbara County, California, noted the burgeoning effects of divisiveness on a community: "[W]e live in a time when divisiveness translates not only into a lack of communication but a basic lack of respect for opposing views, and a growing we-vs.-them animosity." But there are ways to bring communities together to build a future on the resolved differences of the past. In Santa Barbara County, people who disagree on policy issues have joined hands to work together for young people. They are trying, as Cirone puts it, to "form a circle of responsibility around our children."

This chapter examines the process of community development, in which citizens discover ways to work together to improve the quality of life for everyone in the community. This process is presented as a component of the Community Learning Center, which provides a vehicle for making the community development process work.

DEFINING COMMUNITY DEVELOPMENT

In the 1970s, when there were both high interest and federal money for developing model community education programs, an interesting debate developed over the role community education should play in the broader society. I remember one gathering of community education leaders convened for the purpose of defining a clear direction for the movement. Ron Castaldi, then the U.S. Department of Education's designated community educator, facilitated the dialogue. Two distinct views of community education quickly emerged. One view held that community education is really a process of community development; those who held that view supported community-based organizations rather than community schools as vehicles for implementing community education. Opposing them were those who saw community education as a process for reforming the educational system; their hope was that community schools would shift the focus of education outward to encompass the needs and resources of the community.

There was also a small group—and I was among them—who were fence-straddlers. We believed that community schools could be both a force for reforming the educational system and a vehicle for community development.

The issue of community-based vs. school-based community education was not resolved at that meeting, and perhaps never will be. The Community Learning Center model proposed in this book assumes that the community school is a viable vehicle for initiating a community development process, and that better communities will mean better schools.

There are many definitions of community development. For this chapter, I use a definition that has endured over several decades of work in this area. Biddle and Biddle (1965, p. 78) offer this definition: "Community Development is a social process by which human beings can become more competent to live with and gain some control over local aspects of a frustrating and changing world. Personal growth through group responsibility is the focus."

The Biddles developed several operating assumptions from their study of successful community development efforts:

- Each person is valuable, unique, and capable of growth toward greater social sensitivity and responsibility.
- Each person has underdeveloped abilities in initiative, originality, and leadership; these qualities can be cultivated and strengthened.
- These abilities tend to emerge and grow stronger when people work together in small groups that serve the common (community) good.
- There will always be conflicts between persons and factions. Properly handled, conflicts can be used creatively.
- Agreement can be reached on specific "next steps" of improvement without destroying philosophic or religious differences.
- Groups are capable of growth toward self-direction when members assume responsibility for group growth and for an inclusive local welfare.
- When people are free of coercive pressures and can therefore examine a wide range of alternatives, they tend to choose the ethically better and the intelligently wiser course of action.
- A concept of the common good can grow out of group experience that serves the welfare of all in some local area.
- Satisfaction and self-confidence gained from small accomplishments can lead to the undertaking of increasingly difficult problems in a process of continuing growth. (pp. 65–71)

It is fascinating to observe that the Biddles' assumptions, formulated in the 1960s, are still valid.

Compton and McClusky (1980, p. 229) merged the concepts of community education and community development into what they call community education for development (CED), which they define as: "A process whereby community members come together to identify their problems and needs, seek solutions among themselves, mobilize the necessary resources, and execute a plan of action or learning or both." In this formulation, the community is the central focus, providing the environment and social context within which nonformal and informal learning takes place. Compton and McClusky warn that if public school educators unilaterally try to control community education for development, "it is highly unlikely that they will be able to obtain the kind of participation, representation, and coordination necessary to bring about a self-sustaining movement" (p. 249).

My work in support of community development groups has led me to a series of observations about the nature of community development. These observations seem to hold true whether community development is being undertaken by a neighborhood association or a countywide economic development organization.

- Communities do not develop apart from individuals; self-development must be thought of as a part of group development.
- People learn best through self-discovery.
- People work to satisfy human needs.
- To be motivated, people must view a problem as their own: "If there is nothing in it for me, I am not interested." The cost of a solution must be one that people are willing to pay.
- People have among themselves the knowledge to solve their own problems.
- The role of the professional is to help citizens understand and walk through the process.
- Democratic leadership is shared.

DEFINING COMMUNITY

Before exploring the role of the Community Learning Center in community development, we must define community. Noted sociologist Talcott Parsons (1951) described the elements that must be present if a village is to be a community. One of the first is that the village must be a base of operations for carrying out daily activities. George Hillary, Jr. (1955, p. 118), a long-time faculty member in the sociology department at Virginia Tech, believed that a community could be defined as "a social group inhabiting a common territory and having one or more common ties."

The territory served by a Community Learning Center is often defined as the residential area in which the children who attend the Center live. This could be a neighborhood as conventionally defined, or it could be a wider area, perhaps one devised to yield a higher degree of racial balance in the school. In any case, the homes of the children who attend the Community Learning Center are the first dimension of the community.

Using Parsons' first element—"a base of operations"— the Community Learning Center can be a focal point for many community functions. Most important, it can be a place where citizens come together to bring about positive change in the community.

GUIDING PRINCIPLES FOR COMMUNITY CHANGE

If community development is to be incorporated successfully in the Community Learning Center, some guiding principles must be established. In *Facilitating Community Change*, Fessler (1976) produced an outstanding guide to community development. (It should be noted that little has been added to the body of community development literature over the last 10 to 15 years.) Fessler recommends that planned change be initiated where genuine interpersonal communication is possible because of strong identification with a particular community. The service area of a school could thus be defined as a community because its size allows for personal communication.

Fessler's second recommendation is that "the more community problems can be dealt with across institutional lines, free of the domination of any one institution, the greater will be the chances of breaking away from the limitations of the past and arriving at workable solutions that are in the interest of the total community" (1976, p. 13). This point should not be overlooked by educators who see community schools or learning centers as the facilitators of community development: Other community institutions must also be involved and supportive, and solutions should always be sought across institutional lines.

Fessler's third recommendation is that concerned citizens outnumber bureaucrats in the decision-making process. If the reverse is true, Fessler believes, survival of the bureaucracies may take precedence over the needs of the people.

Finally, Fessler believes that, "to the extent that contemplated changes will necessitate establishing new norms of thought and behavior for the community as a whole, it is essential that citizens representing organizations from all socioeconomic levels be included in the decision" (1976, p. 13).

While these guidelines seem fairly basic and even self-evident, experience shows that they are often neglected. Moreover, schools in many communities lack the degree of credibility within the community that is needed to initiate a community development process—especially a process in which citizens are empowered to identify their own problems and seek their own solutions. Credibility has to be built over time; the Community Learning Center will have to demonstrate that it is sincere in its desire to support and facilitate citizens in "doing their own thing" to improve the quality of life in the community.

COMMUNITY REBUILDING

In many cases, the community development process requires rebuilding a community whose infrastructure has been allowed to deteriorate. Schorr (1997, pp. 360–64) makes these observations about successful community rebuilding:

- ♦ Successful initiatives combine action in the economic, service, education, physical development, and community-building domains.
- ♦ Successful initiatives rely on a community's own resources and strengths as the foundation for designing change initiatives.

- ◆ Successful initiatives draw extensively on outside resources, including public and private funds, professional expertise, and new partnerships that bring clout and influence.

- ◆ Effective initiatives are designed and operated on the basis of one or more plausible theories of change.

The Community Learning Center can be a powerful force in the rebuilding of community. To be part of the process, a conscious decision must be made that the investment of resources will have a direct and positive impact on the education of children and young people. A key responsibility of the Community Learning Center is leadership development.

LEADERSHIP DEVELOPMENT

One of the primary tasks in the implementation of community development is the development of community leaders capable of carrying out the process. My mentor, Don Weaver (1979, p. 6), professor emeritus at Western Michigan University, described the kind of leadership needed by professional community educators:

> [L]eadership not only committed to making the world a better place for mankind but…capable of conceptualizing the interrelationships among the elements which comprise community and…trained in the skills required to operationalize the tenets of the community education faith.

The same kind of leadership is needed by those who would lead local community development efforts.

Community members must be helped to develop the skills that they need to work together. Group process or team skills will be the primary building blocks. It is always surprising to find out how many people—even those with advanced education and professional backgrounds—lack the basic skills necessary for effective group activity. All members of the group may need training to assume the diverse roles of facilitator, recorder, manager, and group member; each role is important to the success of a group. As members learn how to fill various roles, they begin to understand the tasks necessary for group effectiveness.

Learning about other group process roles—mediator, consensus seeker, gatekeeper, timekeeper, summarizer, harmonizer, observer—gives group members opportunities to discover new approaches to problem solving and consensus decision-making. Training in the collection and analysis of data prepares community groups for assessing community needs, identifying problems, and selecting potential alternative solutions.

Training can be provided by Community Learning Center staff working with resource trainers from nearby colleges and universities, or from such agencies as the Cooperative Extension Service.

ORGANIZATION FOR COMMUNITY DEVELOPMENT

To facilitate community development, the Community Learning Center staff work with community leaders to form a community development council. This council works closely with the Community Learning Center council but focuses on issues that emerge from the broader community. Leadership of the community development council may be rotated among community members on a regular basis, thereby assuring personal growth opportunities to a larger number of people and avoiding domination of the group by a member or members who assume power and never let go.

The council's agenda comes out of an active needs-assessment process. Community issues that are likely to turn up include:

- Drug trafficking and use.
- Scarcity of employment opportunities.
- Teen pregnancies.
- Lack of affordable housing.
- Limited recreational activities for youth.
- Lack of health services for families and senior citizens.
- Family violence and spouse abuse.

Citizens, acting on their own, may not have the ability to bring about change in any of the areas listed. Typically, the issue under study is brought to the attention of an appropriate community agency or organization, and joint efforts are undertaken to address the problem. This kind of citizen action inevitably makes public service agencies and community institutions more responsive to the needs of citizens.

INCLUSION, NOT EXCLUSION

One caution to keep in mind as community development efforts get underway is that the process must focus on being inclusive. People from every segment of the community—that is, every subgroup identifiable by race, ethnic origin, age, socioeconomic status, employment, or religion—must be involved. It is not enough simply to issue an invitation. There must be a conscious effort to bring people representative of the community as a whole into the process. The result is likely to be a highly heterogeneous group that may well never have been together in that community. At the start, some suspicion or lack of trust may be evident among various segments of the community—for example, the young may distrust the old, African Americans may be uncomfortable with Hispanics and Asians, and Baptists may be wary of Catholics.

The unifying starting point is agreement on a mission: working together to create a better quality of life for all members of the community.

One group that needs special mention is the youth of the community. Too often, people who want to find ways to improve life in the community forget to invite young people to be a part of the process. Groups have been known to sit for hours discussing what they believe young people in the community need without once asking them what they think, or in any way involving them in the dialogue. We underestimate the ability of our young people to contribute to a better understanding of the community and to come up with better approaches to problems.

PATIENCE

Patience is required of anyone who works with the community development process, because it take time to make the process work. Father Gerald Pantin (1984, p. 6), a community educator and community developer from Trinidad-Tobago, writes: "Listening, consulting with the community, having patience to wait and proceed at the pace of the people, these are the skills necessary for community workers wherever in the world they work." Father Pantin's advice, while excellent, is not easy to follow. Professionals often get impatient at the slow pace of communities, and their impatience may tempt professionals to jump in to help the action along. The result may be that the community, rather than seeing this action as helpful, views it as an attempt to take over the process, thus disempowering the community.

We even need to develop a tolerance for failure. To allow a group to fail, but to use the failure as a way to learn and develop, is an effective avenue to real empowerment. It says to the community, we support you in developing your own agenda and taking your own action, even if you are not successful. This does not mean that the staff cannot give advice and share opinions with members of the council, but it does mean that final decisions are left to the council.

I recently studied the issue of leadership in community education in collaboration with two graduate students. The study lead us to four conclusions that are, I believe, applicable to leadership in community development:

> [C]ommunity educators can assist all community members in: (1) becoming increasingly aware of their own leadership opportunities and responsibilities; (2) discovering their power of choice to transform intentions into positive, constructive actions; (3) constantly striving to improve their leadership readiness for more holistic, inclusive, participative approaches to social and education reform; and (4) building the critical mass of people and resources necessary to produce safe, healthy communities across our nation. (Eltringham et al., 1994, p. 8)

REFERENCES

Biddle, William W., and Loureide J. Biddle. 1966. *The Community Development Process*. New York: Holt, Rinehart and Winston.

Compton, J. Lin, and Howard McClusky. 1980. "Community Education for Community Development," in Edgar J. Boone et al., eds. *Serving Personal and Community Needs Through Adult Education*, San Francisco: Jossey-Bass.

Cirone, William. 1995. "Undoing Divisiveness, the Community Way," *Santa Barbara News-Press*, March 26.

Eltringham, R., S. Parson, and J. Skehan. 1994. "The Power of Choice: Reframing the Community Education Leadership Crisis," *Community Education Journal*, xxii, 1.

Fessler, Donald. 1976. *Facilitating Community Change: A Basic Guide*. LaJolla, CA: University Associates.

Hart, Joseph K. 1913. *Educational Resources of Village and Rural Communities*. New York: Macmillan.

Hillary, George. 1955. "Definitions of Community," *Rural Sociology*, 20 (June).

Pantin, Gerald. 1984. *The Servol Village*. Ypsilanti, MI: High Scope Press.

Parsons, Talcott. 1951. *The Social System*. Glencoe, IL: Free Press.

Schorr, Lisbeth. 1997. *Common Purpose: Strengthening Families and Neighborhoods to Rebuild America*. New York: Doubleday.

Weaver, Donald C. 1979. *Leadership for Community Empowerment: A Source Book*. Midland, MI: Pendell Publishing.

9

YEAR-ROUND SCHEDULING

They say that if it were not for air conditioning, Las Vegas would still be a sleepy desert town. Air conditioning may also turn out to be a significant factor in converting our part-time public schools into year-round institutions.

It makes little sense to continue to close public schools for more than two months every summer, perpetuating the charade of having children available to help with the planting and harvesting of crops. We are no longer an agrarian society, driven by the needs of farming—if, indeed, we ever were.

YEAR-ROUND EDUCATION

Since the 1970s, when the National Center for Year-Round Schools was opened at Virginia Tech's College of Education, year-round scheduling in schools has rapidly gained popularity across the country. The number of year-round schools has increased from a handful in the 1970s to 2,681 in the 1997–1998 school year, according to the National Association for Year-Round Education (NAYRE, 1997).

The definition of year-round education offered by Quinlan and Quinlan (1987) is widely accepted by those involved in the year-round education (YRE) movement: "YRE is the reorganization of the school calendar into instructional blocks and vacations distributed across the calendar year, so that learning is continuous throughout the year." (p. 1)

Proponents of year-round education point out that this definition does not increase the number of days in the school year (for example, from the current 180 days to 200 or 220). Worthen and Zsiray (1994, p. 5) make this clear, noting that extended attendance plans, on the other hand, aim at "increasing the educational offering to students by lengthening the amount of time they attend." Worthen and Zsiray note that schools could do both—that is, add school days *and* spread the total number of days across the calendar year; by their definition, such schools would be identified as extended-attendance schools with a year-round education program.

For our purposes, the Community Learning Center uses the term year-round education to describe both the scheduling of instruction throughout the calendar year and the extension of the school year to include more days in school.

STAFF DEVELOPMENT

It has been argued that schools should close in the summer to allow teachers to participate in staff development programs or return to college campuses to work on advanced degrees. But that argument doesn't hold when you realize that business and industry spend far more time and money than schools to provide training for their employees and never close plants and offices for weeks at a time to get the job done.

GROWTH OF PUBLIC YEAR-ROUND EDUCATION IN THE U.S. OVER A 12-YEAR PERIOD

School Year	States	Districts	Schools	Students
1985–86	16	63	411	354,087
1986–87	14	69	408	362,669
1987–88	DATA NOT COLLECTED			
1988–89	16	95	494	428,961
1989–90	19	115	618	520,323
1990–91	22	152	859	733,660
1991–92	23	204	1,646	1,345,921
1992–93	26	301	2,017	1,567,920
1993–94	32	369	1,913	1,419,280
1994–95	35	414	2,214	1,640,929
1995–96	37	447	2,368	1,754,947
1996–97	38	460	2,400	1,766,642
1997–98	38	496	2,681	1,934,060
Growth Rate	138%	687%	552%	446%

U.S. Totals for the 1997–98 School Year:
    States: 41
    Public Districts: 496
    Private Districts: 51
    Public Schools: 2,681
    Private Schools: 71

Statistics compiled by the National Association for Year-Round Education (NAYRE), PO Box 711386, San Diego, CA 92171-1386, (619) 276-5296.

Moreover, an examination of current practice in teacher staff development reveals a shift in the pattern of activities and programs. The state of Virginia, for example, has dropped the requirement that teachers earn a certain number of hours of university credits annually to keep their certification up-to-date. That requirement has been replaced by a point system that offers an array of options for recertification, graduate courses being just one of the options.

Another change that negates the argument that summer breaks are needed for staff development is the trend for colleges and schools of education to offer off-campus graduate programs in the evening and on weekends year-round to provide greater access for teachers. No longer do educators have to travel to the main campus to obtain a degree from many universities. Due to the relatively isolated location of its main campus, Virginia Tech has been a leader in the development of off-campus degree programs since its college of education was established more than 25 years ago.

Distance learning is also a major factor in the changing pattern of staff development. Many programs are available year-round to teachers and administrators through distance learning programs. Satellite broadcast transmissions of graduate courses and workshops has proliferated in recent years, and almost every public school system in the U.S. now has access to a satellite dish or compressed video capable of receiving many of the staff development programs offered. Compressed video, offering two-way video and voice over telephone lines, is fast becoming a major link between public school educators and university faculties who are providing staff development on a wide variety of topics.

Done correctly, a year-round schedule could considerably enhance both staff development and student learning in the Community Learning Center. To comprehend how this would happen, we have to reject the reigning paradigm that describes how schools function and stop thinking in terms of school calendars that deny formal instruction for the majority of students for nearly three months out of every year.

The year-round schedule proposed here, unlike most models currently in place, does not take the traditional 180-day school year and spread it over 12 months through scheduling that allows a school building to serve a larger number of students.

PRISONERS OF TIME

In April 1994, the National Commission on Time and Learning submitted to the U.S. Congress a report with the intriguing title *Prisoners of Time*. Summarizing a 24-month investigation, the Commission listed "five unresolved issues [that] present insurmountable barriers to...efforts to improve learning" in American schools:

- The fixed clock and calendar is a fundamental design flaw that must be changed.
- Academic time has been stolen to make room for a host of nonacademic activities.
- Today's school schedule must be modified to respond to the great changes that have reshaped American life outside of school.
- Educators do not have the time they need to do their job properly.
- Mastering world-class standards will require more time for almost all students. (p. 13)

YEAR-ROUND PLANS

The term year-round education suggests to many people that students in year-round schools are in their classrooms 52 weeks a year. The reality is that most are attending school for roughly the same number of instructional days (175–180) and hours as students who are following a conventional 9-month schedule; the biggest difference is that vacations and classes both occur throughout the 12 months. A few of the more popular year-round plans now in place across the country are described here.

SINGLE-TRACK DESIGN

All students assigned to a school are on the same calendar and are in class or on vacation at the same time. Single-track schedules appear to be the choice of just over 40 percent of year-round models currently in place (799 schools in 1993–1994), according to an unpublished report by the National Association for Year-Round Education (1995). This design replaces one long summer break with a number of shorter vacation periods spread throughout the school year. Some educators believe that this design eliminates much of the need to spend time in the fall trying to bring students back up to speed by reteaching what they had learned before the summer vacation.

MULTITRACK DESIGN

Multitrack schedules place students in groups or tracks, usually four or five per school. Each group has classes the same number of days, and has the same number of vacation days. At any given time at least one track or group of students is out of school while the other students are in school. This design has become popular in communities that are experiencing a major strain on facilities. With a multitrack schedule, a school can serve 25 to 33 percent more students without additional construction or the use of portable classrooms. This design also offers shorter, more frequent breaks, rather than the traditional long summer vacation.

The province of Alberta, Canada, which has experience in multitrack scheduling, reports that this schedule works best when the school enrollment is more than 600 students. "Each track can be considered as a 'school-within-a-school' and each track normally requires the full range of services that are available to the school as a whole" (Alberta Department of Education, 1991, p. 4).

45/15 PLAN

In this plan, the calendar is divided into 9-week quarters of 45 school days each, with each quarter separated by a 3-week (15 school days) vacation. In the 45/15 multitrack plan, students are often divided into four groups or tracks; while three groups attend school, the fourth is on vacation. The groups rotate every 3 weeks, with each group spending 45 days in class and 15 days on vacation. This rotation provides an additional 33 percent of space in the school. According to Ballinger (1990, p. 2), "Teachers usually follow the track schedule of their students; however, they can be reassigned to another track, thereby lengthening their contract year and earning a larger salary." A single-track version of 45/15 is currently the most popular form reported by NAYRE (1997).

60/20 PLAN

This plan is a variation of the four-track 45/15 plan: students are in school for 60 school days followed by vacation for 20 school days. Groups or tracks rotate throughout the year until all have had three 60-day school terms and three 20-day vacations. Ballinger (1990, p. 3) observes that the 60/20 plan "has become a good compromise for those who want longer teacher and student vacation periods." This format is also popular with schools that use a year-round calendar.

90/30 PLAN

In this plan, two 90-day semesters are separated by two 30-day vacation periods. One vacation period comes during the traditional winter holiday period, and the other is in early summer.

CONCEPT 6 PLAN

A popular plan in school systems that have a critical shortage of space, Concept 6 divides students into three groups; at any given time, one group is on vacation. The term Concept 6 comes from the structure of 6 terms of 43 to 45 days each, depending on the number of days required by the state. Some schools choose to extend the number of minutes of instruction each day so that the total accumulation of minutes equals the minimum number of days required by the state. Students attend four of the six terms; two of the four terms must be consecutive (NAYRE 1997).

EMPHASIS OF THESE PLANS

In all of these year-round plans, the emphasis is on saving space in schools with limited facilities. Some evidence can be found that the schools are also motivated by educational considerations, but in the past two decades, increased building capacity has been the dominant reason for starting year-round schools.

YEAR-ROUND EDUCATION IN THE COMMUNITY LEARNING CENTER

The most important difference between the year-round plans described previously and the Community Learning Center's year-round plan is that the CLC plan expands the school year for both the students and the faculty. The traditional school year of 180 class days is expanded to about 210 days. This does not mean, however, that the activities of the traditional school year are simply spread over 30 additional days. Instead, both teachers and students would be involved in different kinds of activities during additional school days. The term "extended school year" might best describe the expanded calendar of the Community Learning Center.

Under this calendar, the school year would begin in August with a 90-day term, followed by a winter holiday break of 15 school days. The second term would begin in January and would consist of another 90-day block of classes. A 15-day summer break would be followed by a 30-school-day (6-week) enrichment term scheduled during the months of July and August. Following the designations used for other optional plans, this one might be labeled 90/15/90/15/30. This schedule would allow time for family vacations during the winter holiday break and before or after the summer enrichment term.

ENRICHMENT TERM

Calling the summer term "the enrichment term" acknowledges its focus on activities and classes designed to supplement the learning program offered during the rest of the year. Individual schedules are prepared in consultation with each student's advisory committee (consisting of a teacher, parents, and a community mentor). Unlike today's typical summer school, the enrichment term is an integral part of the school year; student attendance is mandatory.

TWILIGHT FAMILY LEARNING CENTER
ELK GROVE, CALIFORNIA

The Twilight Family Learning Center program opened in 1993 at one year-round elementary school. Today there are Twilight Centers at four elementary schools in the district. All the schools that house Twilight Learning Centers are open year-round (as are the Centers) and have school-wide Title I programs; all district students and their parents, however, are welcome to attend the programs. The centers offer K-12 homework/tutoring activities, preschool classes, and a variety of classes for adults on Tuesdays, Wednesdays, and Thursdays, from 4:00 p.m. to 7:00 p.m. All the programs emphasize literacy development, and many of the participants are recent immigrants. The activities generally focus on improving student performance through parent involvement, but there is a special emphasis on helping minority students and their families with language skills.

The activities the Centers offer are loosely structured. The largest of the three Twilight Center programs provides students in grades K-12 help with homework and tutoring. Students work in groups of 20 and are supervised by a certified teacher, a teaching assistant, a high school or college volunteer, and a community or parent volunteer. Students who are off-track can participate in reading or math activities at special activity tables. Teachers lead younger children in literacy development activities on the stage of the multipurpose room. Preschool-aged children attend classes based on the Head Start model and focus on pre-reading activities in the schools' kindergarten room. Parents can choose from a variety of classes including ESL (there are large Vietnamese and Latino populations in the district), citizenship, parenting, and adult education that are held in the school's classrooms. All participants take a break at 5:30 p.m. to eat soup donated by Campbells, a large local employer.

(Text continues on next page.)

On a typical night, the four Twilight Learning Centers attract 800 students, parents, and preschool children. All classes maintain a 1:20 teacher-to-student ratio. In addition to the certified teachers, each group of 20 students is joined by high school student volunteers, interns from two local universities (the University of California at Davis and California State University at Sacramento), AmeriCorps volunteers, and community volunteers.

Eighty percent of the program funding is from Title I. Additional funding comes from the Gifted and Talented program and emergency immigrant program funds.

Students who need more time to master the content of an academic course may be given the opportunity to do that. Others may elect to study topics that they have not been able to pursue during the "regular" school year because of time limitations. Still others may choose to become involved in field studies, research projects, community service learning, or internships in the community. The table on the next page offers a sample of enrichment-term programming.

There are variations between the lower and upper grades in the kinds of enrichment programs offered, with modifications dictated by the needs of individuals and groups. Planning for the enrichment term is the responsibility of the Community Learning Center council working with parents, students, staff, and community.

ENRICHMENT-TERM PROGRAMMING

Academic Enrichment	Expanded Horizons	Community Studies	Field Studies
Individually Extended Courses	Technology Applications	Internships in Community Businesses	Environmental Research
Compressed Courses	Performing Arts (drawing on talents of local performing groups)	Community Service Learning	Community Surveys
Seminars in Advanced Topics Taught by Community Resource Persons	Visual Arts (drawing on talents of local artists)	Shadowing Community Mentors in Job Settings	Visits to Historical Sites
Foundation Skill Development (reading and math)	Business Enterprise Development	Studying an Agency or Institution that Serves the Community	Archeological Studies of Local Historical Sites
Study and Test-taking Skills	Work Skills	Genealogical Studies	Recreational Skills

IMPACT ON THE FACULTY

The idea of employing teachers for 12, rather than 10, months often encounters opposition. Educators express concern that schools would lose good teachers who had been attracted to the field because it permits teachers to have summers free to spend with their families. While this is probably true, there are few professions that permit practitioners to take off almost three months a year. And it is probably also true that many more good people would be attracted to teaching if the salaries were higher.

If public school teaching were to become a full-time profession, adding about 17 to 20 percent to annual salaries, it
would begin to compete with other professions that require
similar preparation. This would go a long way toward reducing the frustration of working in a profession that society says
is one of the most important but is also one of the most poorly
paid. An annual salary of $37,000, which is near the national
average, would become a 12-month salary of about $43,000—
not enough by any standard to make teachers wealthy, but
perhaps enough to make teaching more attractive to a larger
number of talented people willing to commit themselves to
rebuilding American public education.

Popular novelist John Grisham (1995), who often writes
about the legal profession, observes, "If lawyers earned the
same salaries as school teachers, they'd immediately close
nine law schools out of ten." (p. 143)

Family vacation schedules always become an issue in dis-
cussions of the school calendar. With a year-round schedule
that allows more frequent breaks at different times of the
year, family vacations could be scheduled throughout the
year, thus accommodating the many Americans who prefer
times other than summer for their vacations.

TAXPAYERS

The greatest opposition to implementation of this year-
round plan would come from taxpayers. In many communities across the country, fewer than 30 percent of households
have children in the public schools. These communities,
many struggling to provide adequate funding for the current
180-day year, will face an enormous challenge in meeting the
cost of extending the school year. One of the keys to accom-
plishing this monumental task is the design of the Community Learning Center. The Center will be a focal point for
learning for all of the community's citizens, young and old
alike. This broadened focus will not only contribute to the development and well-being of the community, but will build
support among those who now have no direct link to public
schools.

The role of individual teachers in the Center may change
from time to time in order to carry out this broadened mis-

sion. For example, reading and language arts teachers might work with undereducated community members during part of the year. (A more detailed discussion of this idea is presented in Chapter 10.) Many teachers are enthusiastic about the possibility of working with adults from time to time. One teacher commented, "Working with adult learners would give me a chance to shift gears and do something that is really needed in our community." It is almost unbelievable that, given the large number of illiterate adults in this country, we have yet to bring into play the greatest resource we have to address their problem—our public schools and the many excellent teachers who work in them.

The National Center for Family Literacy lists four components of a comprehensive approach to family literacy:

- Basic skills instruction for parents or caregivers.
- Preschool or literacy education for young children.
- Regular parent and child interaction.
- Parent education and parent support activities.

The Community Learning Center views its faculty as a resource for meeting the community's educational needs. Teachers move between age groups, going where their skills are needed. This necessitates using some staff development resources to develop a greater understanding of the adult learner.

Year-round operation of the Community Learning Center also facilitates the collaborative delivery of community services to families. With traditional schools virtually locked up in the summer months, many agencies have difficulty maintaining year-round services for families whose needs are unrelated to the school calendar.

IMPACT ON STUDENT ACHIEVEMENT

Many countries have a longer school year than the American average of 180 days. France, for example, has 185 days, Germany has 226 days, and Japan has 243 days (National Association for Year-Round Education, 1995). Many Asian immigrant parents enroll their children in Saturday school programs in the U.S. in order to increase their learning opportunities. The impressive academic performance of many Asian American children may be attributable, at least in part, to the extra help these children receive in Saturday school programs.

The National Urban League has launched a Saturday program in which African American children and their parents work together on hands-on math and science projects designed to be fun while reinforcing the regular classroom instruction received during the school week. This program has also been effective in getting parents involved in their children's learning.

PARENTS AND YEAR-ROUND SCHEDULES

In many communities, parents are the biggest opponents of year-round school schedules. This opposition comes mainly from a reluctance to disrupt child care plans in families in which all of the caregivers are employed outside the home. While the year-round schedule proposed for the Community Learning Center would create child care needs when the schools are on break, the extra days in school would actually reduce the total number of days of child care needed.

Local businesses and other community stakeholders must be involved in an inclusive process of planning for year-round education. Many large employers schedule plant shutdowns during the summer months to permit maintenance and modification of the tools of production, and such shutdowns should be coordinated with school schedules. Often, all this would take is communication between schools and the corporate community—communication that has been lacking in the past.

It may be necessary to phase in the extended schedule over a period of two to three years to minimize the tensions caused by the change. Once implementation of the 210-day extended calendar is complete, most people in the community will quickly forget that there was ever another way to schedule the school year.

The goal in scheduling programs and activities in the Community Learning Center is to provide a seamless approach to education that does not convey the message that education takes place only when students are in classes, and that classes take place only between September and June.

Who Decides?

In too many communities, administrators or school boards, driven by pressures created by the need for additional facilities and the lack of funds to build them, act without input from parents, teachers, or the community to adopt a year-round schedule. When word of what is planned gets out to the community, school board meetings are jammed with angry people opposed to the change.

The key to peaceful change in the school calendar is to offer broad-based involvement early in the decision-making process. The focus should be on creating positive change in teaching and learning. If a proposed change in the calendar doesn't have the potential to improve academic outcomes for students, it will not be worth the time and effort required to carry it out.

In the Community Learning Center, learning will be all-day, year-round, and lifelong for everyone in the community.

References

Alberta Department of Education, Policy and Evaluation Branch. 1991. *Year-Round Education: Some Questions and Answers.* Project Description/Research Based. ED342073. Edmonton, Alberta, Canada.

Ballinger, Charles. 1990. "Year-Round Education: Learning More for Less," *Updating School Board Policies,* 21, 5 (June), 1–5. Alexandria, VA: National School Boards Association. Educational Policies Service, Evaluative Report. ED332274.

Bradford, James C. Jr. 1991. *Year-Round Schools: A National Perspective.* Evaluative Report/Research Based. ED343259.

Brekke, N. R. 1994. "YRE: Its Time Is Now!," *The Year-Rounder,* San Diego: National Association for Year-Round Education.

Grisham, John. 1995. *The Rainmaker*. New York: Doubleday.

National Association for Year-Round Education. 1995. Unpublished report. San Diego, CA.

National Association for Year-Round Education. 1997. Internet: http://www.NAYRE.org.

Quinlan, G. C., and Emmett T. Quinlan. 1987. *Year-Round Education: Year-Round Opportunities: A Study of Year-Round Education in California*. Sacramento, CA: State Department of Education.

U.S. General Accounting Office. 1995. "Cooling Off: Percentage of Schools with Air Conditioning in Classrooms, by State," *Education Week*, May 10.

Worthen, B.R., and S.W. Zsiray, Jr. 1994. *What Twenty Years of Educational Studies Reveal About Year-Round Education*. Chapel Hill, NC: North Carolina Educational Policy Research Center.

10

FAMILY LITERACY AND LIFELONG LEARNING

By the year 2000, every adult American will be literate and will possess the knowledge and skills necessary to compete in a global economy and exercise the rights and responsibilities of citizenship.

Goals 2000, U.S. Department of
Education, 1994

The goal that every adult American will be literate by the year 2000 has seemed unimportant to some of our fellow citizens. We are at times a nation in denial when it comes to admitting that we have illiterate citizens. One of my graduate students recently said, "Oh, the adult literacy goal is an easy one, because it is already accomplished." When I responded that many adult citizens lack the skills to be functionally literate in today's society, she thought I was joking.

My wife had a surprising encounter with illiteracy when she taught biology at a local high school—an encounter that had a major impact on both of us. She had left a note on the blackboard telling the janitor not to sweep her room because of an experiment in progress. She returned from a faculty meeting to find him sweeping. When she asked him if he had seen her note, he said, "I'm sorry, I can't read." He was 25 years old. We tend to assume that illiterate people are members of the homeless, jobless corps that haunt our cities. We don't expect to find adult nonreaders working, especially working in a school.

According to the 1993 National Goals Panel report (1994, p. 47), "Nearly half of all Americans read and write at the lowest levels of prose, document, and quantitative literacy in English" (see *Literacy Levels* figure on next page). While these adults do have some limited literacy skills, they are unlikely to be able to perform the range of complex literacy tasks that the National Goals Panel considers necessary to compete successfully in a global economy and exercise the rights and responsibilities of citizenship. The panel also found that about one-third of all adults took adult education courses during 1990–1991; the other two-thirds said that barriers such as cost, lack of time, and the lack of basic academic skills kept them from taking courses.

Data from the most recent National Household Education Survey (U.S. Department of Education, 1997) indicate that about 40 percent of adults in this country participate in some adult education activity (excluding full-time degree programs). This is an increase over the 33 percent rate found in the 1991 study. Participation (full-time and part-time) in Basic Skill and English as Second Language (ESL) programs rose from 7.8 percent in 1991 to 15.1 percent in 1995, indicating that we are beginning to make slow progress toward meeting the national goal of full adult literacy.

Goals 2000 includes objectives that can serve as points for measuring progress toward meeting the goal of 100 percent adult literacy. If we are going to come anywhere close to attaining that goal, Community Learning Centers across the country must take an active role in working toward achievement of those objectives.

LITERACY LEVELS

■1 = 0-225 points (lowest)
◨2 = 226-275 points
□3 = 276-325 points
▥4 = 326-375 points
■5 = 376-500 points (highest)

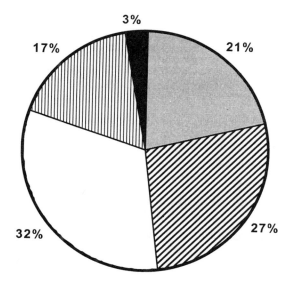

Source: "Local Goals Reporting Handbook,"
National Goals Panel, 1994.

OBJECTIVES FOR ADULT LITERACY
AND LIFELONG LEARNING

+ Every major American business will be involved in strengthening the connection between education and work.

+ All workers will have the opportunity to acquire the knowledge and skills, from basic to highly technical, needed to adapt to emerging new technologies, work methods, and markets through public and private educational, vocational, technical, workplace, or other programs.

+ The number of quality programs, including those at libraries, that are designed to serve more effectively the needs of the growing number of part-time and midcareer students will increase substantially.

+ The proportion of qualified students, especially minorities, who enter college, who complete at least two years, and who complete their degree programs will increase substantially.

+ The proportion of college graduates who demonstrate an advanced ability to think critically, communicate effectively, and solve problems will increase substantially.

+ Schools, in implementing comprehensive parent involvement programs, will offer more adult literacy, parent training, and lifelong learning opportunities to improve the ties between home and school and enhance parents' work and home lives. (National Goals Panel, 1994)

CURRENT LITERACY PROGRAMS

A number of federal, state, and local program initiatives are currently addressing the illiteracy problem. The biggest effort at the federal level is the Adult Basic Education program (ABE), which provides funds to support the delivery of instruction to adults who are functioning below the eighth grade level. The ABE program came about as a result of the Adult Education Act (AEA) of 1966. The federal government spent about $362 million for adult literacy and basic skills education in 1993, more than double the amount spent five years previously (Office of Technology Assessment, 1993, p. 11). But even after doubling expenditures, only small progress has been made in solving the problem.

AEA programs are available without charge to anyone who needs assistance in basic literacy skills or high school completion. The programs focus on educationally disadvantaged adults regardless of their economic or employment status.

A chart prepared by the Office of Technology Assessment (shown below) illustrates how little federal money was directed at adult literacy needs compared to other domestic needs during the 1992 fiscal year.

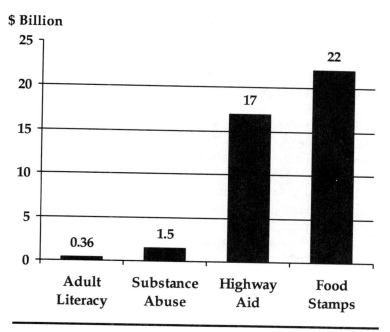

FUNDING FOR SELECT FEDERAL DOMESTIC PRIORITIES, FISCAL YEAR 1992

Vanezky and Wagner (1994) found that federal funding increases have been related to enrollment increases in basic skills classes, but predicted that the likelihood of large increases in the future is small. Their prediction holds up for fiscal year 1997, when AEA programs were funded at just slightly over the $340 million, which represents a flat line pattern of little or no growth over the last few years.

HIGH SCHOOL COMPLETION AND THE GED

In today's economy, credentials are very important in the search for meaningful employment. Even entry-level jobs require a high school diploma or an equivalency certificate. Data from the 1990 census show that 1.6 million (about 11.2 percent) of all 16- to 19-year-olds were high school dropouts. This means that a very significant pool of young people do not have the minimum credentials for entry-level jobs.

Further, the 1990 census reveals that only 75.2 percent of U.S. adults aged 25 and over have a high school diploma. This means that if we define "literate" as having a high school diploma, 39 million adults in this country are not literate.

But using school attainment as an index of literacy may reveal little about what people actually know and can do. The skills of adults with the same level of education vary widely. Many employers complain that our current high school graduates do not have the skills to perform tasks necessary to function at the entry level in today's workplace.

Many communities have programs to prepare adults to take the General Education Development (GED) tests that qualify people for a high school equivalence certificate. A few communities offer adults the opportunity to return to evening classes and complete the necessary course requirements to obtain a high school diploma.

Unfortunately, high school completion programs reach only a small portion of the large number of adults who do not have a high school education. Part of the problem lies in the difficulty of recruiting people who may have had a bad experience with the educational system the first time around. The heart of the problem, however, is the lack of commitment from institutions and the government to make high school completion a priority.

When it comes to adult education, there is no neatly defined system in place to serve the needs of adults. The public schools serve some needs through evening school programs that are often underfunded, understaffed, and inadequately lead. Others involved in the formal adult education programming business include community colleges, universities, and volunteer organizations, but none of them generally see adult education as their primary mission. For each of these institutions, adult education tends to be a secondary mission that is always running in the background.

The Community Learning Center assumes as a mission responsibility for providing for the educational needs of the adults as well as the children and youth of the community. This does not mean that the Community Learning Center will become the programmer for all adult education, but it does mean that it takes an active role in:

- Conducting needs assessments to identify adult education programs that should be offered in the community.

- Establishing partnerships with agencies that offer educational programs for adults (community colleges, labor unions, Literacy Volunteers of America, etc.).

- Providing space for the programs to make them accessible to the community's adults.

- Helping to publicize programs and recruit adult students.

WHAT DO ADULTS NEED TO KNOW?

The U.S. Department of Labor conducted an extensive study to identify the skills necessary for productive entry-level workers. The Secretary's Commission on Achieving Necessary Skills (SCANS, 1990) lists three foundation skill areas:

- **Basic skills**—reading, writing, arithmetic and mathematics, speaking, and listening;

- **Thinking skills**—being able to learn, reason, think creatively, make decisions, and solve problems; and

- **Personal qualities**—responsibility, self-esteem, self-management, sociability, and integrity.

The commission added five workplace competencies:

- **Resources**—knowing how to allocate time, money, materials, space, and staff;

- **Interpersonal skills**—being able to work on teams, teach others, serve customers, lead, negotiate, and work well with people from culturally diverse backgrounds;

- **Information**—being able to acquire and evaluate data, organize and maintain files, interpret and communicate, and use computers to process information;

- **Systems**—understanding social, organizational, and technological systems, being able to monitor and correct performance, and design or improve systems; and

- **Technology**—being able to select equipment and tools, apply technology to specific tasks, and maintain and troubleshoot equipment. (Office of Technology Assessment, 1993)

These specifications for adult learning suggest a foundation for programs designed to prepare undereducated adults for the world of work. Federal programs started since the early 1990s, tend to focus on workplace literacy programs for employed adults. These programs are designed to meet the literacy demands of the job market and "create new workplace/education partnerships that stimulate private sector literacy efforts." (SCANS, 1990, p. 13) As a nation, we cannot afford to have a person try to become a productive member of the workforce who does not have the basic skills to succeed. Members of the corporate community are becoming increasingly willing to enter into partnerships with educators to seek new solutions to the problems of unskilled adults.

FAMILY LITERACY PROGRAMS

In most communities, there are parents who are unable to participate actively in their children's education because of their own low literacy skills. Knowing that higher levels of parental education are linked to better educational outcomes for children, Congress has started to link family literacy initiatives with federal Head Start and Even Start programs, as well as with Title 1 compensatory programs. English as a Second Language (ESL) programs are also getting resources to address the literacy needs of our growing immigrant population.

Family literacy programs aim to help parents or other caregivers improve their own basic skills while they learn new ways to incorporate reading, writing, and communication skills into the lives of their children. The results of these programs are twofold: families improve their lives through increased education, and children's chances for success in school are improved.

Some new programs take an intergenerational approach to literacy that recognizes each adult not as an individual with literacy needs, but as a member of a larger family unit that includes children, spouses, and others. Besides improving the basic skills of individual participants, these programs focus on increasing the use of reading and writing in everyday family life with the children.

An outstanding family literacy model is the Kenan Trust Family Literacy Project, whose primary goal is to break the intergenerational cycle of undereducation and poverty by improving parents' skills and attitudes toward education, improving children's learning skills, improving parents' childcare skills, and uniting parents and children in a positive educational experience.

The Kenan model, which was developed in Louisville, Kentucky, builds on four activities: preschool for children; adult basic education for parents; Parents and Children Together (PACT); and Parent Time (PT). In the morning, parents receive adult basic education instruction while their children attend a cognitively oriented preschool program. Parents and children play together during PACT time, with the adult education and early childhood instructors present to facilitate interaction and learning. During nap time parents meet to discuss subjects such as parenting, child development, home activities, and personal care and growth (Liontos, 1992).

THE COMMITMENT TO ADULT LITERACY

Our society has created an educational system that is full of compartments, barriers, and roadblocks that make it difficult for people to move from one level to another. Our elementary schools serve children beginning at age five, as long as their birthdays come before the first day of December. Then we have middle schools for that magical transition from childhood to adolescence, and high schools where we hope young people will start on a path toward productive adulthood. We have few effective programs to serve those who were failed by the system the first time around.

The Community Learning Center develops programs based on the needs of adults it serves. These programs include everything from basic skill development (ABE) to high school credit courses to job training skills. They are sponsored directly by the Community Learning Center, or other agencies or organizations in the community, who are ready, willing, and capable of providing them.

One of the greatest resources we have for teaching people the basic skills they need to survive in our society is the public schools and the thousands of teachers who work in them. To some it is inconceivable that the very system that failed these people the first time should give them a second chance at learning. But it would be more inconceivable to refuse to make the kinds of adjustments needed in our public schools to be successful with adult learners. Our public schools represent too great a resource to be left out of the war on illiteracy.

On a temporary teaching assignment in Australia, I had the opportunity to visit a high school in the city of Adelaide. One of the striking experiences in that visit was seeing adults who had not graduated from high school in classes with the "regular" students of a traditional high school. I asked how it worked, having adults old enough to be parents of some of the students in classes. One administrator told me it was one of the best things to happen to that school. She reported that student discipline problems related to classroom conduct had almost totally disappeared, and that the students had accepted their new elder classmates with enthusiasm. Teachers in the school reported that the adults in their classes brought real-world experiences that helped enrich the instruction. The school reported a high rate of completion for the adults who were enrolled in the program.

WELFARE TO WORK

New welfare reform initiatives are bringing increased demand for adult education services. The threat of losing benefits significantly reduces the reluctance of welfare recipients to enroll in adult education programs. In a recent study, Wikelund (1993, p. 2) found that a majority of women who were on welfare went back to school only because they would otherwise have lost their welfare benefits, but as the class progressed they developed a variety of other motivations for participating:

> (a) the opportunity to be independent and to find better jobs; (b) their children's well-being; (c) the need to be good role models for their children; and (d) self-improvement. These motivations are in fact very similar to those of adult basic education students in nonwelfare contexts.

Welfare recipients required to move into the workforce need job skills to make themselves employable. By some estimates only one-fourth of the welfare population has the job skills to succeed in the labor market. Another one-fourth needs some job training and basic skills upgrading, and the remaining one-half represent a major challenge to the success of welfare reform because their needs cannot be met through the typical, short-term intervention. (Cohen et al., 1995)

WHAT ABOUT FUN CLASSES FOR ADULTS?

In the 1970s and 1980s, when many community education programs got their start in public schools, there was a great emphasis on getting people into the school. Frank Manley, the father of modern American community education, used to tell his staff at the Flint, Michigan, Community Schools that four I's were needed to assure successful community participation:

+ *In*—get the people of the community into the school, primarily by means of recreation and education.

+ *Interested*—get them interested by explaining problems and asking their help in solving them.

+ *Involved*—ask people to help. They are willing and able [to help] when given the opportunity.

+ *Informed*—an informed person is a responsible citizen concerned with improvement. (Flint Board of Education, 1969, p. 9)

During that era some critics criticized the quality of the community involvement espoused by community educators. Warden (1974, p. 2) gave voice to that indictment:

> The major difficulty occurs when community educators move from the realm of philosophy into the world of practice. Many Community Education programs have gotten people IN the schools only to have their involvement end at this point. The sad resulting fact has been too often [that] Community Education is still basically identified as a series of school-sponsored programs and projects.

Community involvement occurs at all points in the process of developing programs in the Community Learning Center. This involvement will come not only through formal representation on decision-making councils, but through an ongoing dialogue that must take place in the community. That dialogue is an important part of the way the Community Learning Center relates to the community it serves.

While some "fun" adult education programs are important for the social development of community members, they should not consume all or most of the resources and energies of the Community Learning Center. There are generally plenty of organizations and agencies in every community who are ready, willing, and capable of providing for the avocational needs of the adults in the community. The YMCA and YWCA, park and recreation departments, and many private providers are capable of providing many of the kinds of programs and activities that people want. The role of the Community Learning Center is to serve as a broker for the community, bringing agencies with programs together with community members who want or need to participate. The Community Learning Center is capable of providing places where these programs are accessible to those who want to participate.

If they don't have to spend time and energy developing cake decorating classes and basketball leagues, community educators working in the Community Learning Center can be free to help the community focus on problems critical to the survival and growth of the community and the people who live there—problems such as family literacy and preparation for the world of work.

The Community Learning Centers being developed as part of the New American Schools Project by Designs for Learning (1995, p. 44) in St. Paul, Minnesota, have adopted this policy for their centers:

> Centers should be open year round and many hours a day, with classes offered at various times to accommodate individual learner's work schedules and biological clocks. There should be access to child care and comfortable places within the Center for the adults to meet and socialize. Attempts should be made to link teams of providers with business and industry to provide needed services and to show relevance of subjects to the real world.

The Community Learning Center defines learners in a much broader way than schools of today typically do. Learners are the residents of the community from the very young to the very old. Lifelong learning will become a reality as a broad spectrum of learning needs is addressed by all the available resources in the community.

REFERENCES

Designs for Learning. 1995. *Community Learning Centers: Design Specifications*. St. Paul, MN.

Liontos, Lynn B. 1992. *At-Risk Families and Schools Becoming Partners*. Eugene, OR: ERIC Clearinghouse on Educational Management, University of Oregon.

Kozol, Jonathan. 1985. *Illiterate America*. New York: Doubleday.

National Goals Panel. 1993. National Goals Report, *Task Force Report in Assessing the National Goals Relating to Postsecondary Education*. Washington, DC: National Goals Panel.

Office of Technology Assessment. 1993. *Adult Literacy and New Technologies*, Washington, DC.

11

LEADERSHIP IN THE COMMUNITY LEARNING CENTER

Staffing and leadership in the Community Learning Center are inseparable concepts. The staff should consist of a wide variety of people, both career professionals and community volunteers. Everyone in the Community Learning Center should have an opportunity, and be encouraged, to assume leadership. This chapter examines a variety of staff roles, including principal, community linker, teacher, parent, and community partner.

WHAT SHALL WE CALL THE PRINCIPAL

While writing this book, I had a conversation with Don Gresso, a professor of educational leadership at East Tennessee State University and coauthor of an excellent book on school leadership. As I described a new vision for schools called Community Learning Centers, Gresso asked me what title I was recommending for leaders of these centers. Retaining the title of principal risks having people assume incorrectly that the leadership role would be the same as that currently found in the traditional school. Our search for a new title ranged from director to facilitator to lead teacher, but none seemed to exactly fit. Until we can come up with an option, one that accurately conveys a role consistent with the new community learning centers, I will continue to call the lead person in the center the principal.

PRINCIPAL

The position of Community Learning Center principal is perhaps the hardest to describe because of our firmly entrenched views of what principals do and how they do it. In many schools, the principal has traditionally served as a transactional leader, maintaining control of resources and having the power to decide how the school should operate. In the past, successful principals seem to have functioned as "benevolent dictators," often rewarding teachers for supporting administrative decisions by providing them with additional resources for their classrooms or favoring them in scheduling decisions. Most of these principals showed a preference for focusing on administrative issues that did not directly involve teaching and learning issues. An experienced principal once stated that all she had to do to keep everyone happy was to tend to the five "B's": bathrooms, boilers, buses, ballgames, and beans (translated to mean the cafeteria).

The new leadership model proposed for the Community Learning Center calls for a transformational leadership style that is directed toward developing the potential of those involved in the work of the center, whether they be paid staff, volunteers, or students. In a study of the principal's role in restructuring schools, Leithwood, Jantzi, and Fernandez (1994, p. 80) provided a list of the characteristics of transformation leadership style that would have the principal function as the facilitator of a process designed to empower people in the school community to grow in their abilities to exercise shared power.

Transformational Leadership
- Vision building
- Group goal consensus
- Modeling
- Providing individual support
- Providing intellectual stimulation
- High performance expectations
- Contingent rewards

Another emerging leadership pattern for principals is described by Goldman, Dunlap, and Conley (1993, p. 70). Called facilitative leadership, this behavior is demonstrated by:

(a) Creatively overcoming resource constraints of time, funds, and information; (b) maximizing human resource synergy by building teams with diverse skills and interpersonal chemistry; (c) maintaining sufficient awareness of staff activities to provide feedback, coordination, and conflict management; (d) spanning boundaries to create intra-school and community networks that provide recognition; (e) practicing collaborative politics that emphasize one-on-one conversation rather than large meetings; and (f) through these behaviors, modeling and embodying the school's visions. Principals use these tactics to solve student learning problems, create an environment for school restructuring, and build staff instructional and leadership capabilities.

Murphy and Beck (1994, p. 15) give an excellent description of what would be expected of the principal in a Community Learning Center:

Principals must be able to forge partnerships and build strategic alliances with parents, with businesses, and with social service agencies. They must lead in efforts to coordinate the energy and work of all stakeholders so that all the children in the schools are well served.

QUALITIES AND SKILLS OF COLLABORATIVE LEADERS

Everyone in the Community Learning Center needs to develop the qualities and skills of collaborative leadership. While it is difficult to identify all of the many skills involved in collaboration, the following is a partial list:

- Vision building
- Communication (especially listening)
- Group process
- Conflict management
- Consensus building
- Risk taking
- Flexibility and openness to new ideas

It will not be enough for the principal alone to have these skills. They must be developed among all the members of the staff of the Community Learning Center if the environment of sharing and collaboration is to become a reality, and not remain just a theory.

COMMUNITY LINKER

In the early models of community schools, there was a staff position called the community school director or community education coordinator. Minzey and LeTarte (1994, p. 260) recommend that a "community school program have at least one full-time, trained community educator to coordinate and direct the effort." The Flint, Michigan, model of community education showcased to the nation in the 1970s and 1980s had a community education director in every school building.

As the position evolved in many community schools, community educators became increasingly identified with developing and operating programs in the school. They became adult education programmers, recreation planners, and education-enrichment developers, even as community education theorists urged them to adopt a "process" orientation. Minzey and LeTarte's *Community Education: From Program to Process* (1972) described a process that focused on citizen involvement in community problem-solving and needs assessment that would lead to the development of programs in community schools. Unfortunately, many top administrators of the school districts that housed the community schools either did not understand the process role or did not support it. Process, being less tangible than programs, was difficult to assess. School-based community educators felt pressured to produce programs as tangible evidence of their efforts, and community schools, sometimes regarded as "programmers of last resort," expected to develop programs that other agencies were not ready, willing, or capable of providing.

In the Community Learning Center, one staff position is designated the Community Linker. This person should be a trained community educator responsible for providing leadership to link the Center to the community. The presence of the community educator in the Center does not mean that others on the staff won't share in that important work, but it does mean that there will be one person who will take the primary leadership in seeing that the job gets done.

Many traditional schools pay lip service to the components of the Community Learning Center: parent and community involvement; collaborative community service delivery; use of community resources in the instructional program; extended use of school facilities by the community; and life-long learning. The difference often comes down to a matter of staffing commitment. Few traditional schools are making the kind of staffing commitment to ensure that these kinds of things happen in the school, regardless of how much the leaders of the school say they value them. If a staff person does not have major responsibility for seeing that certain things happen, such as genuine parent and community involvement, it often doesn't happen.

The position of community linker (many other titles might fit this position, but the term "linker" graphically describes the function) is the person responsible for maintaining the process functions of the Community Learning Center and assuring their effectiveness. These process functions include:

- ◆ Involving the community in the operation of the Community Learning Center.
- ◆ Supporting community development.
- ◆ Increasing the use of the community as a class-room.
- ◆ Developing a climate for the self-actualization of all community members.
- ◆ Facilitating collaboration among community agencies to help community members solve community problems.
- ◆ Maximizing use of the Community Learning Center facilities by the community.

In some parts of the country, the community school linker or community education staff, is jointly supported by the school district, community service agencies, and the local government. This approach assures that the staff can work on issues that relate to social, cultural, health, or recreational issues that are the realm of nonschool agencies, as well as to issues and problems directly related to the educational mission of the school.

In 1972, Weaver completed a national study of the goals of community education. A review of those goals today offers insight into the role a contemporary community school linker might play in the Community Learning Center. The goals supported by respondents in the Weaver (1972) study were:

- ◆ Coordination
  - Coordinates effort of community agencies.
  - Provides effective communication.
  - Eliminates duplication among agencies.
  - Helps residents secure educational services.
  - Provides a forum for community problems.
- ◆ Surveying
  - Identifies community problems.

- Surveys attitudes and interests.
- Identifies required resources.
- Demonstration
  - Demonstrates humanistic approach to education.
  - Demonstrates methods of social change.
  - Provides model of community living.
  - Demonstrates principles of educational leadership.
- Programming
  - Extends use of school facilities.
  - Increases multiage and cross-cultural contacts.
  - Provides programs for senior citizens.
  - Provides teenage enrichment and recreation.
  - Provides recreation programs.
  - Provides high school completion programs.
  - Improves educational opportunity for minorities.
- Training
  - Develops leadership among lay citizens.
- Promotion
  - Increases participation in existing school programs.
  - Promotes school as primary education agency.
  - Improves public image of the school.

The goals for community education produced by Weaver's study provide a template for the kinds of demands that are placed on the staff of the Community Learning Center.

TEACHERS

The role of the teacher in the Community Learning Center require a set of characteristics very different from those currently used to recruit teachers for traditional schools. Because the Community Learning Center will have, as a matter of principle, a collaborative culture, teachers who join its staff must be ready to be a part of that kind of culture. Many teachers now working in traditional schools long to be able to move out of a restrictive environment to one in which they can have a more significant role in the overall leadership of the school.

IMPACT II–The Teachers Network is an organization of teachers who are working to help create the kind of climate proposed for the Community Learning Center. IMPACT II's president, Ellen Dempsey (1995, p. 4), writes:

> The future is here. The world that we knew as recently as 5–10 years ago no longer exists. Teachers standing in front of a room of passive students lecturing them—transmitting information fragmented into discrete disciplines—belongs to the past. The challenge for today's teachers is to facilitate learning and to be leaders in our complex, often overwhelming information age.

Teachers in many schools have been isolated and powerless in determining the changes made in their schools. The Community Learning Center change the balance of power by including teachers in the important task of providing leadership.

Ann Lieberman (1995, p. 6), codirector of the National Center for Restructuring Schools and Teaching (NCREST), observes that a changed role for teachers will not come without conflict:

> As teachers begin to take leadership in the restructuring of schools, creating new curricula, expanding their repertoire of instructional strategies, and using new assessment techniques, they will inevitably become involved in conflicts and challenges. These come, in part, from teachers assuming new roles where they are no longer simply "implementing" someone else's ideas, but are becoming creators and inventors with their own ideas of how to better provide for student learning. They also ap-

pear as teachers try to create cultures of collaboration to replace the ubiquitous culture of isolation.

Teacher's isolation can be seen in classrooms that are closed off from "outsiders," even if those outsiders are their own peers.

A collaborative culture will not happen just because someone thinks it is a good idea. Lieberman (1995, p. 21) provides a list of the currently accepted norms in school life that will have to be challenged:

- ◆ Teachers expect to be alone.
- ◆ Support, like time, is limited.
- ◆ Learning is for students, not necessarily for adults.
- ◆ Knowledge comes from experts, not from local initiative.
- ◆ Leadership is synonymous with the principal.
- ◆ Routines are good, while change is risky.
- ◆ Inventions are for inventors, not teachers or schools.
- ◆ Reforms will come and go.

To make teacher leadership a reality, the Community Learning Center challenges these norms by making fundamental changes in the way we have looked at teachers and their roles in schools.

STUDENTS

Unfortunately, students are usually thought of as raw material to be processed in the school (factory) and transformed into productive members of our society (products). In the Community Learning Center, students are active workers in the teaching and learning process. On occasion, they will be involved in cross-age tutoring, teaching younger students things they have already learned, following the old proverb, "To teach once is to learn twice."

Don Weaver has been interested in student involvement in the educational process for more than 30 years. Writing in the *Michigan Journal of Secondary Education,* Weaver (1971) was intrigued by the student unrest that occurred on college and high school campuses as a result of conflicts over the U.S. role in Vietnam during the 1960s. He saw that a shift was taking place among students who were becoming more aware of societal conditions, but observed that schools were not changing to accommodate this new awareness in their students. According to Weaver, "even in the secondary schools beset by the same social and organizational problems which plague the society outside the school, there is a reluctance to do other than 'play school' through the promotion of the innocuous activity program typical of secondary school student councils over the past 50 years"(p. 36). If students are to be constructively involved, he wrote, their involvement must rest on certain basic principles:

- There must be a provision for school personnel to learn from students.
- The school staff must provide expertise in the procedural aspects of decision-making.
- Students must be considered as equal partners in the process.
- Student leaders must be trained.
- There must be a schoolwide plan for involvement that is clearly understood by all students and regularly includes all students in discussion of issues. (pp. 38–41)

Clearly these principles are relevant to the kind of institution the Community Learning Center strives to be. A true learning community requires that everyone involved be both teacher and learner. The decision-making system proposed for the Community Learning Center in Chapter 4 provides for involvement of students and for the development of the kinds of skills needed to participate in that process.

One other point to consider in a discussion of student involvement in staffing the Community Learning Center is a student role in keeping the facility clean and functional. Schools in Japan have a tradition of routinely involving students in the cleaning and maintenance of school buildings.

Students are expected to pick up trash, wash blackboards, and dust floors. It would seem that we could find a way for our students to become more involved in this manner. It should not be an issue driven by a desire to save money, although it might have the potential to reduce some maintenance costs. It should be a strategy to for developing a greater sense of pride and ownership in the school.

There is one image that has stayed with me from my own experience as a student in a Midwestern urban high school. My sophomore class was the first to attend school in a brand-new building. Mr. Hutchins was the school's soft-spoken principal. Every day he could be seen in the cafeteria picking up trash from the floor, clearing abandoned dirty dishes from the tables, and talking with students. At first I thought that Mr. Hutchins was providing a wonderful example as he cleaned up messes left behind by careless students. I think I expected the students to be embarrassed by having the principal clean up after them—so embarrassed they would then take care of their own messes. I was wrong. It soon became clear that most of the students were perfectly happy to have someone to clean up after them. They seemed to have no investment in having a clean place to eat because Mr. Hutchins was there to do it for them.

What would we have learned if our principal had involved the student body in a discussion of the role of students in maintaining a clean and pleasant environment in the school? As it was, we did learn a lesson; but unfortunately, it was that there will always be someone there to pick up after you. And, of course, we all learned later that it was not true.

One other aspect of student involvement merits attention and concern. Weaver (1969) points out that conflict in the secondary schools had created a focus on the legal aspects of students' rights, with the result that *extralegal* rights were relegated to a position of secondary importance. He notes that "it is in the provision for the guarantee of *extralegal* rights of the student that the school demonstrates its interest in helping the student to become a fully-functioning, self-actualizing member of society" (p. 24). Weaver suggests that the extralegal rights of students include:

- The right to make mistakes and thereby to learn.
- The right to be taken seriously.
- The right to know the specific expectations held for [the student].
- The right to be accepted as a citizen with all the rights pertaining thereto.
- The right to a share in the control of [the student's] environment.
- The right to be involved in substantive issues relating to [the student's] education—the curriculum, the schedule, the methods of instruction and the cocurricular program.
- The right to a relevant curriculum—one from which [the student] can make some sense. (p. 24)

It is interesting to see how relevant Weaver's 1969 ideas are in the context of our secondary schools in the 1990s. The extralegal rights he enumerated become the foundation for the way individuals relate to each other in the Community Learning Center, whether they are students, teachers, administrators, or community members.

LEADERSHIP TRAINING

During the 1970s and 1980s, the Charles Stewart Mott Foundation supported an extensive network of centers that trained persons in leadership positions in community education. The centers were located in universities, state departments of education, large urban school districts, and a national center in Flint, Michigan. The training was both pre-service and in-service, and sometimes led to graduate degrees.

The Mott centers and many of their programs disappeared as the Mott funding declined and virtually vanished in the 1990s. Another reason for the disappearance of community education training was the lack of employment opportunities in schools. Although schools continued to talk about the values of community education, they were unwilling to invest resources in the staff positions needed to support those values. As jobs for community educators disappeared, the programs to prepare them were closed down.

The major remaining resource for training staff for the Community Learning Center is the National Center for Community Education in Flint, Michigan. With an endowment from the Mott Foundation, the center is able to provide low-cost short-term training through programs mainly conducted at the center. The size and scope of those programs limit the total number of people who can be trained each year. This void in leadership training must be addressed in the coming decade if Community Learning Centers are to become a reality.

HIGHER EDUCATION PARTNERSHIPS

The gap between higher education and public K-12 schools seems to grow ever wider, as the schools have been criticized in recent years. Many in higher education, both education faculty and their colleagues in other disciplines, are guilty of viewing problems in the schools as having little to do with them and what goes on in their classrooms. In reality, education is an integrated system, whether we want to acknowledge it or not. What happens in one part of the system has impact on all the other parts of the system.

It should be noted that the term higher education is used here to include the wide array of postsecondary institutions that exist in most communities: four-year colleges, universities, community colleges, and technical schools.

Fortunately, there has been an awakening among many leaders in higher education. Faculty in colleges of education are forming partnerships with schools that bring them into closer interaction with the challenges that schools face. In universities, faculty members from disciplines ranging from computer science to the humanities, are beginning to realize that the quality of the students they receive is highly dependent on the quality of the K-12 programs in the schools that prepare them.

One of the keys to developing partnerships between higher education and the schools seems to be the creation of opportunities for representatives of both groups to sit down and discuss their common needs and concerns. Another important factor is the dedication of resources to facilitate partnership development. For higher education faculty, working with public schools in a close partnership arrangement is not part of the university's traditional expectations of them. Resources for travel, graduate student support and equipment purchase would serve as incentives for faculty to explore possible actions. The box on the next page lists some recently observed partnership activities.

The Community Learning Center develops an active program of higher education partnerships. Leaders in the Center take the initiative in facilitating dialogue on the needs of the Center and the higher education institutions, and the resources available to bring about real win-win situations for all parties. Higher education institutions recognize and provide support for the role of faculty members who are working in partnership with the Community Learning Center.

If true partnerships are formed with higher education agencies, the Center will have access to a wide array of resources that can extend and enrich learning opportunities for all members of the learning community. The colleges and universities will, in turn, have access to real-world settings in which to provide new experiences for faculty and students. The real winners in these partnerships are the learners in the communities served by the Community Learning Center.

COMMUNITY PARTNERSHIPS

Educators realize that the task of preparing young people to become productive citizens in our complex world is beyond the resources of the school acting alone. Leadership from the community is important for bringing about positive change in our schools.

Community partnership is a vehicle for engaging community leaders in the work of the school. These partnerships may be formed in the business community to support School-To-Work programs, which provide job-based work experience, mentorships, and in-service education for teachers, and to assist in the upgrading of school equipment.

SOME RECENT SCHOOL–HIGHER EDUCATION PARTNERSHIP ACTIVITIES

- Collaborative action research teams working on school-based problems.
- K-12 teachers and administrators serving as clinical faculty in teacher and administrator preparation programs.
- Computer science students working with schools to assist in developing computer networks.
- Collaborative programs preparing school leaders at the graduate level.
- University faculty serving on school improvement councils.
- K-12 personnel serving on university councils and committees.
- College students doing community service learning projects in schools tutoring students.
- K-12 schools serving as professional development schools where teachers and administrators receive their pre-service training.
- Collaboration in staff development programs for both university faculty and K-12 faculty and administrators.

Other partnerships can involve community leaders in curriculum development aimed at improving student achievement. Virginia educators are currently developing community partnerships designed to help students meet new standards of learning that have been put in place by the state to assess student achievement. These partnerships will enlarge the resource base that schools have available to help students meet the high expectations established by the state.

In other examples of community partnerships, schools have joined with community organizations such as the YMCA and YWCA, Cooperative Extension Service, and Rotary Club, to work on specific projects or programs aimed at increasing student achievement. One criticism of community partnerships that must be acknowledged is that many have not been well planned or directed toward student learning. To have the kind of impact needed to address the challenges that face today's schools, partnerships must be focused, well planned, and the evaluated regularly in terms of specific goals.

The National Association of Partners in Education (NAPE) has developed an excellent model for partnership development. Training in how to use the model is provided at many locations throughout the country. Trained leadership will be needed in the Community Learning Center to develop and sustain effective partnership with the community.

REFERENCES

Barth, Roland. 1990. *Improving Schools from Within.* San Francisco: Jossey-Bass.

Goldman, P., D. Dunlap, and D. Conley. 1993. "Facilitative Power and Non-Standard Solutions to School Site Restructuring," *Educational Administration Quarterly*, 29 (1), 69–92.

IMPACT II. 1995. *How We Are Changing Schools Collaboratively.* New York: IMPACT II–The Teachers Network.

Institute for Educational Leadership. 1994. *Preparing Collaborative Leaders: A Facilitator's Guide.* Washington, DC.

Leithwood, Kenneth, Doris Jantzi, and Alicia Fernandez. 1994. ".Transformational Leadership and Teachers' Commitment to Change," in *Reshaping the Principalship,* J. Murphy and K. S. Louis, eds. Thousand Oaks, CA: Corwin Press.

Lieberman, Ann. 1995. "Collaboration: Looking Beneath the Surface," in *How We Are Changing Schools Collaboratively,* New York: IMPACT II–The Teachers Network.

Minzey, Jack D., and Clyde E. LeTarte. 1972. *Community Education: From Program to Process.* Midland, MI: Pendell Publishing.

Minzey, Jack D., and Clyde E. LeTarte. 1994. *Reforming Public Schools Through Community Education.* Dubuque, IA: Kendall/Hunt Publishing.

Murphy, Joseph, and Lynn G. Beck. 1994. "Restructuring the Principalship: Challenges and Possibilities," in *Reshaping the Principalship,* J. Murphy and K. S. Louis, eds. Thousand Oaks, CA: Corwin Press.

Weaver, Donald C. 1969. "Competent Leadership for an Explosive Era." *Michigan Journal of Secondary Education,* 10, 4 (summer).

Weaver, Donald C. 1971. "A Plan for Student Involvement," *Michigan Journal of Secondary Education,* 12, 3 (spring).

Weaver, Donald C. 1972. *The Emerging Community Education Model.* Presidential address, National Community School Education Association (now National Community Education Association), Flint, MI.

APPENDIX

RESOURCES FOR COMMUNITY LEARNING CENTERS

Community Networks: Lessons from Blacksburg, Virginia. Andrew Cohill and Andrea Kavanaugh, Editors; 1997. Boston: Artech House Telecommunications Library; http://www.bev.net

Designs for Learning. Wayne Jennings, 1355 Pierce Butler Route, St. Paul, MN 55104; http://www.anoka.k12.mn.us/transform/Designs.htm (training and program design for community learning centers)

National Association of Partners in Education, 901 North Pitt Street, Suite 320, Alexandria, VA 22314; http://www.napehq.org/ (training, program design and advocacy for educational partnerships)

National Association of Year Round Education, P.O. Box 711386, San Diego, CA 92171-1386; http://www.NAYRE.org (a nonprofit organization that advocates the improvement of K-12 education through implementation of alternative schedules)

National Center for Community Education, 1017 Avon Street, Flint, MI 48503; http://www.nccenet.org (offers training to assist groups and individuals in developing approaches for more effective working with their communities)

National Center for Restructuring, Education, Schools, and Teaching, P.O. Box 110, Teachers College, Columbia University, New York, NY 10027; (212) 678-3432; http://www.tc.columbia.edu/~ncrest (supports restructuring efforts by documenting successful initiatives, creating reform networks, and linking policy to practice)

National Community Education Association, Starla Jewell-Kelly, Executive Director, 3929 Old Lee Highway, Suite 91-A, Fairfax, Virginia 22030

National Health and Education Consortium, c/o Institute for Educational Leadership, 1001 Connecticut Avenue, NW, Suite 310, Washington, DC 20036 (resources in the area of school-based health centers)

National Network of Partnership Schools, Dr. Joyce Epstein, Director, Center on School, Family, and Community Partnerships, Johns Hopkins University, 3303 North Charles Street, Baltimore, MD 21218; e-mail: nnps@csos.jhu.eud; (410) 516-8818 (provides support for schools, districts, and states that are committed to developing and maintaining comprehensive programs of school-family-community partnerships)

REAL Enterprises, 115 Market St., Suite 320, Durham, NC 27701; (919) 688-7325 (provides training and technical assistance to schools interested in starting rural entrepreneurship programs through action learning)

San Diego New Beginnings, San Diego City Schools, 4100 Normal Street (Rm. 2220), San Diego, CA 92103 (a working example of community service agencies working together to serve the needs of children and families)